SHEPHERDING THE SHEPHERD

DEVOTIONS FOR A PASTOR'S SOUL

LEE ECLOV

Publisher: Rob Toal
Editorial: Andrew Finch
Marketing: Todd Watermann
Interior Design: Jillian Hathaway
Cover Design: Rick Szuecs

For Pastor Dave Spooner, my good shepherd

Acknowledgements

My pastor friends helped me write these letters, though they rarely knew it. I listened to our conversations, read their emails to me, gathered with them when I could. As is so often the case, they are fine shepherds and probably don't even know it.

I'm especially indebted to my two editors. First, my wife, Susan, who knows whether or not there should be commas in this sentence and who knows how to be properly picky with what I write. Then, Andrew Finch, who receives most of these pieces just in the nick of time, buffs them up, and dispatches them to more people than I can imagine.

Table of Contents

Introduction

Shepherds in pictures are invariably calm. They stand relaxed while their sheep munch away. They stroll at an easy pace while their flock follows along agreeably. No one ever paints a shepherd in tears or about ready to clobber some recalcitrant sheep with their crook. You never see one trying to fend off sheep who've turned on them nor one bloodied by wolves. They always look brave and tireless. On the other hand, we don't often see shepherds laughing the way pastors so often do, especially when they're together. It's hard to capture in a picture how much shepherds love their flocks, and their joy in simply feeding them or being among them.

I began writing these weekly letters to shepherds in the spring of 2020, and you know what a messed up year that turned out to be. I don't have to remind you just what pressures church leaders faced. My one goal, week after week, was to encourage God's good shepherds, who are my very favorite people.

I imagined how much some shepherd-reader would love to have an old pastor like me just to talk to, someone who wasn't glib or grouchy telling them what to do. I learned quickly to find a Scripture text to gather around so I could be sure that the Lord would be part of our time together.

When someone asks me what I do in retirement I tell them that I mostly try to befriend pastors. That's why I wrote these letters.

Be ye glad!

Pastor Lee

Watch Night

My Dear Shepherds,

In the rural church where I grew up we always "prayed in the new year" in a watchnight service. We'd gather around 9pm for games and food. As midnight approached we moved to the sanctuary where we'd kneel on the cold plank floor taking turns praying till the big hand moved past twelve. This custom was begun by John Wesley in 1740 as a Covenant Renewal Service.

A different strain of watchnight services began for African American churches on the night before Abraham Lincoln signed the Emancipation Proclamation on January 1, 1863. They call it Freedom's Eve.

Christians are meant to live in a watchnight frame of mind. Listen to what Jesus told us:

> *Be dressed ready for service and keep your lamps burning, like servants waiting for their master to return from a wedding banquet, so that when he comes and knocks they can immediately open the door for him.* (Luke 12:35-36)

Watching for Jesus is our pastoral duty. We're expected to have the Master's household ready to welcome him, to be sure no one's lounging in sweats or taking the long night off. All the lights on. All hands on deck to welcome the Master back to his household.

This past grueling year shows how fast catastrophes can engulf the world. Jesus warned that such cataclysmic events will become common as his return approaches. They are not the end times but they are not just *any* times either. Pastors remind God's weary and anxious people, "Jesus is coming back soon! Let's be sure we're ready!"

When Jesus comes in glory no door will be closed to him. No one will sleep through the triumphal shout or the trumpets. So what does Jesus mean when he warns us to be ready to open the door to him?

Throughout Luke 12, Jesus taught his disciples that being prepared means we "publicly acknowledge him before others," and that we stop pursuing "an abundance of possessions" or worrying about food or clothes, but rather to be "rich toward God. . . For where your treasure is, there your heart will be also." That is how we keep our people ready during this long night of watching.

But to prepare our church we must also remind them often, in full biblical detail, that Jesus will come back in glory. Pastors grace God's people with the stories of what is yet to come. We keep their chins up, looking for Christ's return. In this clinging and cloying world we urge them not to put down their roots.

I imagine a pastor being like an elderly uncle of refugee children. He often gathers them to himself and tells them stories of the homeland they have never seen. He tells them that on the day they go home they will be a beautiful bride coming down the aisle of the skies to meet her Bridegroom. The homeless children listen wide-eyed as he tells them that their homeland is a kingdom bright and righteous, where Life runs in the rivers and grows on trees. "Our King is the king of all kings," says the uncle. "He rides a mighty charger and the armies of heaven follow him. He knows your name and he himself is waiting to be with *you*." The uncle tells these stories again and again because if he doesn't the children will forget who they are and put down their stakes in Babylon. The challenge isn't how to get them home. The King will take care of that. The uncle's challenge is that he cannot let the King's children forget their home.[1]

---

[1] Lee Eclov, *Pastoral Graces: Reflections on the Care of Souls* (Chicago: Moody Publishers, 2012), p. 147.

Fingerprints

My Dear Shepherds,
For 22 years I served as Senior Pastor of the Village Church of Lincolnshire, with a Sunday attendance of about 175. In all those years that number didn't change much. That, for me, was a problem because I could not escape the sense that my success as a pastor depended on our church getting bigger.

The competition was tough. I'd tell friends, "I pastor in the land of the giants"—huge, multi-campus congregations all around us. To be perfectly honest, I never really wanted to *pastor* a big church, I just wanted to *preach* to a lot of people. But we never even made it to two services.

When I came to the church I assumed that if I did my job well God would give the increase and, in a way, he did. We had unusually high turnover, sometimes 20 percent in a year, mostly due to students, corporate transfers, and retirees coming and going. Generally, people didn't leave because they were unhappy. During one five-year stretch we lost 261 people in our church directory and we gained 261. We were always saying goodbye and hello.

Instead of bemoaning the constant farewells of wonderful brothers and sisters we had to have a healthier perspective, so I reminded our people again and again that we were putting our fingerprints on all those folks. They'd go on to other churches in other parts of the world taking with them the unforgettable touch of our congregation.

Some of my leaders felt I wasn't aggressive enough in reaching out to the community. Perhaps they were right. I still smart over a comment from one leader I very much respected who told me of another church's growth and then said bluntly, "I'm embarrassed by our church." Yet usually, when I fretted over our situation, our elders pointed to all the signs of health and God's blessing. Our people loved Christ and served one another. We took holiness seriously and prayed together. Visitors often said, "This feels like home."

Ever so slowly I learned to be content. Church size, I'm certain, is overrated and is surely a damaging benchmark for pastoral success. While it is necessary to evaluate our reach and our welcome, pastors are called primarily to be shepherds and the tasks of shepherds are to feed, lead, and guard the flock God has entrusted to us, not the ones he hasn't. I often hearken back to something Dallas Willard said:

> Pastors need to redefine success. The popular model of success involves the ABCs—attendance, buildings, and cash. Instead of counting Christians, we need to weigh them. We weigh them by focusing on the most important kind of growth . . . fruit in keeping with the gospel and the kingdom.

I confess that I always harbored the hope that one day, if we remained faithful, people would just start coming through our doors in bunches. We'd just stand back and be amazed. But when I came to retirement in 2020 that had never happened.

In recognition of my retirement our people gave us a wonderful "Fare Lee Well" evening. At its conclusion Susan and I were given a large, framed picture. When we pulled back the covering it was a two-foot-high thumbprint—mine, actually. Then we were told to look very closely at the whorls, loops, and arches of the fingerprint and there in tiny type were the names of over 1000 people who had been part of our congregation during those 22 years! At the bottom was the inscription, "Thank You for Leaving Your Fingerprints on Us."

No two ministries are alike, I know, but take heart, dear brothers and sisters. Be filled with the Spirit and remain faithful with the Word. Leave your fingerprints, and Jesus', on them.

Is the Father Ever Proud of Me?

My Dear Shepherds,

A question started nagging me after I'd been in ministry a while: *Is my Father ever proud of me?* The question wasn't rooted in my past. My folks were always kind and affirming. Actually, it was Jesus' own words that weighed heavily on me. In Luke 17:10 he said of servants, "So you, when you have done everything you were told to do, should say, 'We are unworthy servants; we have only done our duty.'" And Luke 12:48, "From everyone who has been given much, much will be demanded; and from the one who has been entrusted with much, much more will be asked." I would labor on as faithfully as I could but still I wondered and yearned for God's pleasure.

After I'd prayed and worked hard on a sermon I'd wonder, did Jesus *like* it? Did he like how I explained a difficult part or how the conclusion came together? When I listened well and responded wisely in a counseling session, did he think, "Nice job"? When I managed my frustrations in a meeting and was kind instead of abrupt, did he smile with satisfaction? Maybe being proud of me isn't the best way to put it, but that's how it settled in my mind.

These days it hasn't been easy for pastors to take much pride in your own work. Perhaps you've watched helplessly as your people fought or as they suffered. Maybe you've wondered if you'll have anything to show for all your work. A lot of pastors have never felt so weak or so unfruitful. I remember thinking that I'd like to hear Jesus say, "Well done, good and faithful servant," *now*, when the uncertainty and inadequacy weighed so heavily on me.

When Paul thanked God for the Thessalonians he pointed to "your work produced by faith, your labor prompted by love, and your endurance inspired by our hope in our Lord Jesus Christ." There's no way God heard Paul's thanksgiving and thought, "Dial it back, Paul. They're just servants doing their duty." And so it is for you, dear shepherds.

Remember what God told Samuel, "The LORD does not look at the things people look at. People look at the outward appearance, but the LORD looks at the heart."

It may have taken a pandemic, but I suspect a lot more pastors are "lowly and contrite in heart" now than in the past. Such hearts are God's second home. Shepherds have had little else left but to focus on simply finding ways to care about the souls of their weary and wandering sheep. For that, our Good Shepherd is grateful. When you were wounded by your own congregation, you were sharing in Christ's suffering and he welcomed your company. Even when your prayers were frail and frightened the Lord was glad to be sought. When you took up your Bibles to find your way forward in the fog, the Lord was pleased. In all these things, the Lord no longer calls us servants, but friends.

How could one who loves us so deeply as our Father, who gave his one and only Son to save and transform us, who dispatched his own Spirit to empower, gift, and teach us, and who called us to serve his beloved people, how could he *not* delight in our earnest work for Jesus? If we, being sinful, delight in seeing our children at their best, how could our Father not be proud of us?

Cutting the Heads off My Highness

My Dear Shepherds,

"Every morning I try to cut the heads off my highness—like Medusa," Irma said that to me one morning. She is a Catholic believer, an immigrant, and a cancer survivor, among other important things. She often served me my coffee and a bagel. Medusa was the evil Gorgon in Greek mythology whose hair had been turned to writhing, venomous snakes. I'd never heard our daily struggle for humility put so vividly.

A lot of pastors I know seem to have gotten unwelcome help chopping the heads off their highness. Churches have a dubious reputation for buzz-cutting pastoral pride. But even when our flock is wonderful, shepherding is mostly humbling. I sat in a circle of about 20 solo pastors recently as they talked about the trials of recent months. Many had seen God working but they were also a pretty beleaguered bunch. I didn't hear any bragging.

Pastoral ministry subjects our egos to crazy highs and lows. For example, folks occasionally call me a man of God which, frankly, gives me the heebie-jeebies. I want to be, don't get me wrong, but hearing it out loud seems like asking for trouble. People defer to us for all kinds of things. We speak for God, for goodness sake! It can all go to our heads. On the other hand, I so often felt my ministry was choking in the weeds of my weaknesses.

Eugene Peterson wrote, "The strongest sign of authenticity in what you and I are doing is the inadequacy we feel most of the time." Inadequacy is a necessary qualification for ministry because it keeps the heads of our highness cut short.

Think of Jesus' Beatitudes. God's blessing in each of those is not attached to a virtue but a weakness—poor in spirit, mourning, meekness, famished for righteousness. From those emerge humble virtues: mercy, pure in heart, peacemakers, and the persecuted. These Godward weaknesses render us child-sized in the kingdom. The picture of

Jesus inviting children to come and be blessed is for *us*. It is no small thing to become child-sized.

Lowliness, once you crawl there, is a safe place, a Sabbath for our souls where strivings cease. There is relief and blessing in being small.

I'm all for "he must increase," but the "I must decrease" part doesn't come so easily. High heads are not so easily shorn. That's why James tells us how to cut the heads off our highness:

> *Submit yourselves, then, to God. Resist the devil, and he will flee from you. Come near to God and he will come near to you. Wash your hands, you sinners, and purify your hearts, you double-minded. Grieve, mourn and wail. Change your laughter to mourning and your joy to gloom. Humble yourselves before the Lord, and he will lift you up.* (James 4:7-11)

The uplifting of God is nothing like the pedestal of man. Like Jesus' yoke, God's uplifting is easy to bear, deeply fulfilling, and never precarious. He bestows Christlike credibility upon us. We become better shepherds, safer for the sheep we lead. The hard part is waiting for his lift.

Singing from Parched Throats

My Dear Shepherds,

Conflicts and threats drive our hearts into arid places. It is good and pleasant when brothers and sisters dwell together in unity, but it is terribly dry and dreary when they don't. I spoke with pastor friend recently who was at his wit's end over immovable leaders and he was ready to move from push to shove. But what I heard gasping beneath his frustration was his thirsty heart.

King David prayed Psalm 63 "when he was in the Desert of Judah," fleeing from his rebellious son Absalom. Trauma and turmoil had drained the shepherd of Israel. Out of that terrible desert he gave us this prayer like a holy canteen for our hearts.

> *You, God, are my God, earnestly I seek you;*
> *I thirst for you, my whole being longs for you,*
> *in a dry and parched land where there is no water.* (Ps. 63:1)

Another friend, a pastor's wife, hard-pressed by conflict and criticism, tries to hold back bitterness. Her heart, too, is parched. What's so easy to miss when the Absalomites are hard upon us is how thirsty we've become for God himself. The drier the landscape the more we need the Living Water.

I imagine David sitting on some sun-blasted rock, head down, lost in thirsty prayer. I suppose he lamented this terrible turn of events. I suppose he cried out for God's protection and vindication. But then he entered into a kind of Tent of Meeting. "I have seen you in the sanctuary and beheld your power and glory," he whispered. For our part, we look upon the Cross, the empty tomb, and our Intercessor at the right hand of God.

David in that hour did not know what would become of him. But whether his life would be cut short or stretch on, he prayed as we can,

> *Because your love is better than life*
> *my lips will glorify you.*
> *I will praise you as long as I live,*
> *and in your name I will lift up my hands.* (vv. 3-4)

I imagine it took David some praying to get those words, "your love is better than life," from head to lips. So plan to take your time. Whatever songs David sang, I suspect he had to sing them a few times before they took hold. But sing he did. And so must we. No, really; you *have* to *sing*. Not just read lyrics. Not just review your theology. Not just listen to a playlist. We have to *sing*.

> *I will be fully satisfied as with the richest of foods;*
> **With singing lips my mouth will praise you.**
> *On my bed I remember you;*
> *I think of you through the watches of the night.*
> *Because you are my help,*
> **I sing** *in the shadow of your wings.* (vv. 5-7)

That psalm is a prescription for gripping God in the fierce storms of shepherding.

Long ago I came to love the old hymn, "Spirit of God, Descend Upon My Heart." I have the lyrics taped in the back of my Bible. Each verse is rich, but I have often prayed this one in the dry times.

> *I ask no dream, no prophet ecstasies,*
> *No sudden rending of the veil of clay,*
> *No angel visitant, no opening skies;*
> *But take the dimness of my soul away.*

Badlands

My Dear Shepherds,

"I had assumed that the energy would keep coming. Why wouldn't it? Isn't that what pastors are supposed to do? Stoke the fires? Prime the pump? Charge the batteries? Do the 'American' thing? After only three years was I already a failed pastor?" Eugene Peterson said that, according to a new biography by Winn Collier. Peterson called that period of his pastoral ministry "the badlands," after the barren Dakota territory his family drove through every year traveling from their church in Maryland to Peterson's home in Montana.

Pastors draw energy from promising and interesting challenges—a new discipleship strategy, a surge in visitors, young believers eager to grow, the next sermon series. But sometimes the rains don't come.

Pastor Paul charged Timothy and all of us in the strongest terms possible:

> *In the presence of God and of Christ Jesus, who will judge the living and the dead, and in view of his appearing and his kingdom, I give you this charge: Preach the word; be prepared in season and out of season . . .* (2 Tim. 4:1-2a)

It's the "out of season" part that takes such a toll. The interminable drought. My wife and I spent our seminary internship in a blistering, un-air-conditioned summer only a few miles from the badlands, in Rapid City, South Dakota. Temperatures every day sat in the mid- to high-90s, nary a drop of rain, and the wind blew relentlessly. We had to cancel the hay ride we'd planned for the youth group because the rancher couldn't spare a couple bales of hay. Sometimes pastoral life is like that—"out of season," when opportunity *isn't* knocking.

I've heard that fifty percent of pastors want out. Sometimes God is in that but while you have my heartfelt sympathy, I need to remind you of what Paul said:

> *Preach the word; be prepared in season and **out of season**; correct, rebuke and encourage—**with great patience and careful instruction**. . . . But you, keep your head in all situations, **endure hardship**, do the work of an evangelist, discharge all the duties of your ministry.* (vv. 2, 5)

Just so we're clear, "great patience" means absolute longsuffering, endurance. "Endure hardship" means to suffer evil or afflictions. Peter said, "To this you were called, because Christ suffered for you, leaving you an example, that you should follow in his steps" (1 Peter 2:21). We can't just quit.

I write these things reluctantly because my heart goes out to you. I have heard some of your stories. I know pastors' hearts are breaking and strength is failing. Some of you have borne devastating attacks not only from our enemy but from God's own people. Perhaps you have fallen. Shepherding is harder than we ever imagined, isn't it?

After a solid month of that life-draining drought, rain clouds loomed over the Black Hills to the west. My wife and I jumped in our old VW Bug, rolled down the windows, and headed for the hills, in the opposite direction of the badlands. Big raindrops plopped on the windshield. We stuck our heads out the windows while I drove and laughed as our faces caught the rain.

> *And the God of all grace, who called you to his eternal glory in Christ, after you have suffered a little while, will himself restore you and make you strong, firm and steadfast.* (1 Peter 5:10)

Refreshing Hearts

My Dear Shepherds,

"You, dear brother, have refreshed the hearts of the Lord's people," wrote Paul to Philemon. As you know, Paul had a big ask of his old convert and colleague: grace for his runaway slave, Onesimus. Today, let this phrase rest upon you like a benediction:

> *You, dear brother [or sister], have refreshed the hearts of the Lord's people.* (Phm. 1:7)

It could seem that refreshing the saints is a kind of pastoral extra, like remembering to send your grandmother a birthday card, nice to squeeze in between the big stuff that dominates ministry. But we underestimate how weary, lonely, and thirsty our people often are.

Years ago, a strange headline in the *Chicago Tribune* caught my attention: "City tries to pump up its crews down under." It was a story about a pep rally for the 800 employees of the Chicago Sewer Department. It's a tough job, and the new head of the department gave them a rousing speech. "Winning is not a sometimes thing," he shouted. "It's an all-the-time thing!" (Who knew there was a contest going on down there!) A photo showed a big banner on the wall behind him that said in huge letters, "Bringing Sewers Above Ground."

I often thought of that story on Sunday mornings while I watched folks find their seats. I'd think about the dirty, difficult places where my people worked every week. Some offices are filthier than sewers. Some schools are darker than tunnels. A lot of believers spend their week trying to keep the gunk off their hearts, trying to keep their souls from smelling like a cesspool.

We draw the refreshment we pour forth from the Spirit's well springing up within us. Paul commended his old friend Philemon, "I hear about your love for all his holy people and your faith in the Lord Jesus"

(v. 5). There's our well: love for them and faith in the Lord Jesus. Apart from that whatever we offer is stagnant.

On the sidelines during football games you always see those people whose sole job seems to be squirting Gatorade into players' mouths to restore their electrolytes and keep them hydrated. Our ministry is like that. We circulate among our people—in person, emails, cards, and prayer—offering grace, fresh from Jesus to the spent and parched. When I look back on 40 years of pastoring, I think the best part was simply refreshing the hearts of the Lord's people. Like Paul to Philemon, that is what they thanked me for.

Ours is remarkable work, a wonder really, but it is not too great a stretch for any of us. It isn't dependent on our schooling, age, or personality. It *does* matter, however, that we actively trust Jesus to use us. It does matter that we love the people we meet. It does matter that we shoulder our people's burdens, share in their joys, honor their dignity, and thank God for their fellowship. It does matter that we linger and listen, and that we wait for the Spirit's prompting before we speak. It matters that we attend to our own souls and that we ourselves are refreshed by Jesus."

This particular aspect of our work is not only Christlike, it is heavenly. Revelation 7:17 says that in the kingdom to come, the Lamb "will be their shepherd; he will lead them to springs of living water." Until that day, good shepherds here will always "refresh the hearts of the Lord's people."

'And Playing the Role of the Father . . .'

My Dear Shepherds,

Aw shucks. Just doin' my job. Twern't nothin'. Loved doin' it. That's probably how most pastors would react if told, as Paul told Pastor Philemon, "You, brother, have refreshed the hearts of the Lord's people." But then Paul's compliment took a hard turn because Paul asked Pastor Philemon to forgive his runaway slave, Onesimus, who was likely an indentured servant who had run out on his debt. What's more, Paul wanted Philemon to welcome Onesimus into the Colossian church as a brother in Christ, since he'd become like a trusted son to the Apostle Paul. It was a lot to ask, even of grace.

Paul was asking Pastor Philemon to play out the story of the Prodigal Son on the platform of his church, with Philemon himself in the role of the father. The script said to throw his arms around the wastrel and to summon everyone to celebrate "this son of mine who was dead and is now alive." God does that to pastors sometimes. Our stories won't mirror this one exactly but they're similar enough for us to nod in recognition.

Read Paul's letter to Philemon and you'll root for Onesimus, the reformed runaway. That's the thing, isn't it? Grace looks so good, so right and noble, when you're looking in on a story, but if you're in the middle of it, *grace costs.* Someone has to pay for grace. Our Lord Jesus did, of course, but it costs us too. That goes with taking up his cross ourselves. We, too, play the role of the father.

All Christians are expected to extend grace, but for pastors it is an occupational hazard. I dare say, we get hurt by God's people more than most, plus we are always being watched. Philemon had to play out his part with the whole church watching. Our own performance, whether public or hidden, sometimes requires us to minister to people who have hurt us deeply, who have falsely accused us, or tried to discredit us.

In order to refresh hearts, we must absorb the wound and surrender our grudges to Jesus. We write off their debt. We aren't noble enough to do that apart from the Spirit's help. We meet the Lord alone, pouring out our heartache, detailing the cost. We humbly admit to the plank in our own eye. We recognize that, even in this pain, God's sovereignty is at work. Paul had the audacity to say, "Perhaps the reason he was separated from you for a little while . . ." (Separated?! He absconded!) ". . . was that you might have him back forever—no longer as a slave, but better than a slave, as a dear brother." For Philemon, that might have been a big step of faith.

Paul asked Pastor Philemon, the refresher of the Lord's people, to "refresh my heart in Christ" (v. 20) by welcoming Onesimus back. Whether or not your congregation knows your struggles, they will benefit from the outcome. Grace gains strength, I think, when the price is high, when it has been poured out like that costly nard Mary poured on Jesus' feet. Grace quietly pervades a church with its fragrance, changing the atmosphere, delighting the disciples. It makes churches safe.

Imagine Philemon reading his letter aloud to the Colossian Christians. You could have heard a pin drop. Then surely Philemon walked over to Onesimus and threw his arms around him. I imagine there wasn't a dry eye in the house and the Communion meal that followed was a feast no one ever forgot.

The grace of the Lord Jesus Christ be with your spirit. (Phm. 25)

The Company We Keep

My Dear Shepherds,

Woven through my 70 years are other pastors, many treasured, a few lost. But I would not be the pastor I am, maybe not a pastor at all, without them. I thought of them as I caught the names Paul included in his letter to Philemon.

He greeted Philemon, "our dear friend and fellow worker." Paul had evidently led Philemon to Christ and then entrusted him with the fledgling Colossian congregation. Writing his name must have brought a flood of memories like those I have of beloved brothers and sisters who have shepherded alongside me.

Then at the end of the letter, Paul named his companions in Rome,

> *Epaphras, my fellow prisoner in Christ Jesus, sends you greetings. And so do Mark, Aristarchus, Demas and Luke, my fellow workers.* (vv. 23-24)

You recognize those names, of course. Epaphras first brought the gospel to Colossae (Col. 1:6-7), his hometown. Paul's letter to the Colossians had been delivered along with this personal letter to Philemon. There he wrote,

> *Epaphras, who is one of you and a servant of Christ Jesus, sends greetings. He is always wrestling in prayer for you, that you may stand firm in all the will of God, mature and fully assured.* (Col. 4:12)

I have pastor friends like that. Unsung spiritual heroes who fight for their churches and who know what matters most.

For a biblical example, let's look at Mark, otherwise known as John Mark. He was probably the young man who fled naked from the Garden of Gethsemane the night of Jesus' betrayal (Mark 14:51-52). He also bailed during Paul's first missionary journey (Acts 15:37-40) but eventually regained Paul's trust and confidence (2 Tim. 4:11). Peter also regarded him as "my son" (1 Pet. 5:13). Two steps forward, one step back, but faithful in the end.

Aristarchus was Paul's long-time traveling companion, through thick and thin, and a prisoner with Paul (Col. 4:10). Luke, "our dear friend, the doctor" (Col. 4:14), who alone would be with Paul at the end (2 Tim. 4:11) when all others were gone.

Then there's Demas, the heartbreaker. Here, a good and trusted brother, but in Paul's last letter he told Timothy, "Demas, because he loved this world, has deserted me" (2 Tim. 4:10). I've not been deserted like that but I have known some who have deserted Jesus.

Oh, and Onesimus, the restored fugitive. Around 100 AD Ignatius, the bishop of Antioch, was arrested and sent to Rome to face the wild beasts. At one stop on his journey to Rome, the church in Ephesus sent a delegation with their bishop to encourage Ignatius. Soon after, Ignatius wrote them a letter that still survives. He thanked them for sending their bishop "whose love surpasses words . . . I pray that you may love him with a love according to Jesus Christ, and that you may all be like him."

That Ephesian bishop's name was Onesimus. It's possible it wasn't the same Onesimus, but the timing fits. Onesimus' predecessor there was Timothy, another spiritual son of Paul. Ephesus and Colossae weren't far apart. Not only that, many scholars believe that the first time the letters of Paul were collected was around 100 AD, in Ephesus where Bishop Onesimus led the church. Which could explain how this little gem of a letter that changed the life of a fugitive named Onesimus found its way into the Scriptures.

Perhaps there's a colleague who would be encouraged to hear from you.

Call Your First Witness

My Dear Shepherds,

Maybe this doesn't describe you right now but I picture all pastors at one time or another standing alone and forlorn, hands hanging at their sides, shoulders sagging, bags under their eyes, slack-jawed, with a what-just-hit-me look. I love being a pastor but it can be a brutal business sometimes.

I thought of that as I read Paul's account in 2 Corinthians of the grim pressures he had faced. Talk about tough ministry! Take a look again at his crushing curriculum vitae in 2 Corinthians 6:4-10. He prefaced that list of woes by saying in verse 3, "We put no stumbling block in anyone's path, so that our ministry will not be discredited."

That's our deep desire too—that in whatever we must face, our ministry for Jesus Christ will not be discredited. Some of you have faced demoralizing assaults on your ministry credibility. Most of us have endured times so dark that we couldn't tell if anything at all would be salvaged from our service. Reflecting on times like that Paul wrote,

> *Now this is our boast: Our conscience testifies that we have conducted ourselves in the world, and especially in our relations with you, with integrity and godly sincerity. We have done so, relying not on worldly wisdom but on God's grace.* (2 Cor. 1:12)

It isn't always wise to appeal to our own conscience. It can be merciless and cruel, a grim-faced inner Pharisee, a graceless judge. On the other hand, our consciences can be conned into deadly self-righteousness. But when trained, tempered, and employed by the Holy Spirit, your conscience may be the only fair witness of your conduct. Other belligerent or insinuating voices may be living in your head rent free but close the door on them and listen to your Spirit-sensitive conscience for a few minutes.

When you think back over the chaotic or painful time you've endured, how did you *conduct* yourself, especially among your own flock? Paul pointed to his own integrity—his "moral holiness." In other words, he had behaved under pressure in a manner befitting a man of God. Secondly, he knew he had exhibited godly sincerity, which literally means transparency. His motives had been pure and clear. You could see through him to Christ.

How? How do we do that? Most pastors I know serve Christ with integrity and pure motives. But heavy pressure throws off our internal compass. So how did Paul keep his sense of direction? "We have done so," he says, "relying not on worldly wisdom but on God's grace."

Dear weary shepherd, I know you may not find your conscience so reassuring as Paul did. I don't either. I'm ashamed of some of my behavior. But the grace of God has been displayed in our lives despite our frustrations and folly. Paul began this letter exalting in God's comfort (*parakleseos*—coming alongside). That is the grace that met Paul, and that has met you and me. In your trouble, God has come alongside you, whether you felt him or not. You shared together in suffering for Christ's church.

Once, a dear sheep of my flock came to me in tearful distress. Her job—her calling—had been upended by her boss' decision and she sat with me in the throes of confusion and anger. As I listened to her and Jesus, I settled on some simple counsel. Perhaps it will help you too, in keeping your conscience clear when you don't know what else to do. Three things: Stay small. Trust Jesus. And don't sin.

Yes and Amen

My Dear Shepherds,

At our wedding the pastor (my brother-in-law) insisted we use the old phrase, "I pledge thee my troth," explaining that it meant our vows were forever after tied to our reputations as truth-tellers. That is true for pastors as well. Our word is our bond. When we open the Scriptures, we pledge our troth.

When Paul was prevented from coming to Corinth as he had promised, his critics evidently accused him of not being a man of his word, and that cast doubt on his preaching of Christ. Paul came out swinging:

> But as surely as God is faithful, our message to you is not "Yes" and "No." For the Son of God, Jesus Christ, who was preached among you by us—by me and Silas and Timothy—was not "Yes" and "No," but in him it has always been "Yes." For no matter how many promises God has made, they are "Yes" in Christ. And so through him the "Amen" is spoken by us to the glory of God. (2 Cor. 1:18-20)

We must *always* speak and act with integrity and Christlike transparency lest our God-given gospel message lose its ring of truth. But more than warning, Paul's words ought to have us clearing our throats and counting the hours till the next time we get to open our Bibles.

Who among us hasn't imagined joining Jesus' walk to Emmaus as "he explained what was said in all the Scriptures concerning himself," setting his companions' hearts afire? Now Jesus has entrusted that incendiary privilege to us, whether we are holding up the grand covenants and prophecies given to Abraham, Moses, David, Isaiah, and the others, or we are showing our people the more personal promises tucked all over Scripture. When I was a boy in Sunday School we sang, "Every promise in the Book is mine." I'm not sure that's exactly true, but I'll tell you this: every promise in the Book is Jesus'!

Jesus did the Yes work. What we do in preaching, counseling, and discipling is the Amen work. The Hebrew word means *surely* or *truly*. Jesus Christ is the Guarantor. We are his Amen Corner.

Years ago I was invited to read Scripture in an ordination service at an African-American church pastored by a friend. Just two verses, Isaiah 61:1-2. When it was my turn I opened my Bible and intoned, "The Spirit of the Sovereign Lord is upon me."

The congregation stopped me dead in my tracks: "Amen! That's right! Amen!"

After I found my place again I forged on, ". . . because the Lord has anointed me to *preach* good news to the poor." I punched the word *preach* a bit and there it came again: "*Preach* the good news! Amen! Preach!"

I girded up my loins and marched boldly onward. "He has sent me to BIND UP the brokenhearted." Rolling back like an echo from heaven, God's people shouted, "Bind UP!" "Praise God!" "Thank you Jesus!"

I declaimed, "To proclaim FREEDOM for the captives," and some laughed for the joy of it. Some clapped their hands.

"And release from DARKNESS for the prisoners." Again, they ran out to meet the Word with palm branches and hosannas.

"To PROCLAIM the year of the Lord's FAVOR and the day of vengeance of our GOD."

"Yes! Hallelujah!" Feet stomped on the wooden floor. The congregation burst into applause—*applause!*—for the greatness of the commission.

I closed my Bible and stood there amazed. And I wished like everything they'd given me more than two verses to read.

Yes and Amen!

Letters of Recommendation

My Dear Shepherds,

A pastor friend told me that when he candidated at his church years ago a leader told him stories of several previous pastors, each painted in dark terms. Ever since, he's imagined that when he leaves he will also be the bad guy of his story, no matter what actually happens. In a recent D.Min. class on conflict, his professor asked him, "Who writes your story?"

> "They do," he replied.
> "No," his prof replied.
> He tried again, "I do?"
> "Nope."
> Having no options left he said, "God?"
> "Right," replied his professor. "God writes your story."

Paul's critics in Corinth had created a story about him, saying that he came and left without any proper letters of recommendation. To which he replied:

> *You yourselves are our letter, written on our hearts, known and read by everyone. You show that you are a letter from Christ, the result of our ministry, written not with ink but with the Spirit of the living God, not on tablets of stone but on tablets of human hearts.* (2 Cor. 3:2-3)

How would you reply to someone who said to you, "We're going to need to see your letters of recommendation"? How about saying this:

I have two with me. One is here, inside my jacket, written on my own heart. You're welcome to read it. It's the story of Jesus' work among my flock written into my life. Our fellowship with one another and

Christ in Communion services and church socials is written there. Our prayers are there; you can catch a whiff of the incense. The way my heart rejoiced when I baptized people that summer afternoon at the lake or our wonderful Easter morning services—those are all written on my heart. All that bound us together—"one Lord, one faith, one baptism, one God and Father of us all"—the worship services, the burdens we carried together, they are all there.

You see those tearstains on my letter? They're part of the story, too. Sometimes God's people break the hearts of his shepherds. I've felt them hurt each other, and been wounded myself. And, oh, when those I had worshipped and worked with walked away from our church I just died inside. Sometimes I was just so tired. When my people wept, I cried with them. All that is written there. That's the letter of recommendation here in my inside pocket.

I have another letter. It's a matter of public record. Christ himself wrote it, the Spirit of the living God was his ink, and the hearts of these people I serve are his parchment. My role? Like Mother Teresa said, "I'm a little pencil in the hand of a writing God . . . ." We didn't try to hammer holiness into the people. That never works. It's grace or nothing. While I preached, organized Bible studies, found teachers for the kids, counseled the harassed and helpless, comforted the dying or grieving—all the things pastors do—the Holy Spirit was inscribing God's new covenant across their hearts so clearly, so indelibly, that anyone could read it there. That's my story. That's my letter of recommendation.

> *For what is our hope, our joy, or the crown in which we will glory in the presence of our Lord Jesus when he comes? Is it not you? Indeed, you are our glory and joy.* (1 Thess. 2:19-20)

Grave Dwellers

My Dear Shepherds,

A record number of pastors have thought about quitting over the last year. No wonder. It's been a killer season. I surely don't need to reiterate the reasons. Recently I read and reread the litany of Paul's soul-crushing trials in 2 Corinthians 6:3-10. Good grief, did that man suffer! But he just couldn't quit. He wrote, "Since through God's mercy we have this ministry, we do not lose heart." How was that possible?

> *For God, who said, "Let light shine out of darkness," made his light shine in our hearts to give us the light of the knowledge of God's glory displayed in the face of Christ. But we have this treasure in jars of clay to show that this all-surpassing power is from God and not from us.* (2 Cor. 4:6-7)

Adam was nothing but lifeless clay until God breathed into him the breath of life. No watching angel would see him inhale and remark, "Wow, that's some clay!" No, that's some Breath! So it is with us. Whereas Moses once veiled the fading glory of God after he had been in the Tent of Meeting, the glory of God in Christ radiates permanently and increasingly from within our pottery selves. It's just that we feel so ... clay-ey.

Paul knew the feeling. He said he was hard pressed on every side, perplexed, persecuted, and struck down. He said, "We always carry around in our body the death of Jesus." I wasn't really prepared for that part of ministry: the killer pressures, the confounding expectations, the toxic critics, the demoralizing failures. I didn't factor in my own old nature undercutting me and my weaknesses hobbling me. But that is what dying is like. Believe it or not, those times are how God stages his resurrection power in us. He schedules us for frequent visits to Jesus' tomb.

While despair sometimes accompanies dying (it did for Paul), we are able to be death-to-life models.

> *We are hard pressed on every side, **but not crushed**; perplexed, **but not in despair**; persecuted, **but not abandoned**; struck down, **but not destroyed**. We always carry around in our body the death of Jesus, **so that the life of Jesus may also be revealed in our body**.* (vv. 8-10)

The secret of turning from our tomb is to look again on the glory of our resurrected Christ until our faces shine and our clay inhales Spirit. In his sermon on 2 Corinthians 3:18 over 100 years ago, Alexander Maclaren said, "It is not mere beholding, but the gaze of love and trust that molds us." He continued, "You have been trying, and trying, and trying half your lifetime to cure faults and make yourselves better and stronger. Try this other plan. Let love draw you, instead of duty driving you. Let fellowship with Christ elevate you, instead of seeking to struggle up the steeps on hands and knees. Live in sight of your Lord, and catch His Spirit."

Pastor Josef Tson, a Romanian pastor and educator, suffered terribly under the Communists before the fall of the Iron Curtain. After one particular cruel bout with an interrogator he was very discouraged. Then the Lord met with him giving him a Christlike perspective. The next week the interrogation began again but everything was different. His interrogator stopped and said, "Mr. Tson, who visited you this weekend? I have in front of me a different person than the one who left here. Somebody came and changed you completely. I have to know who came and visited you."

"Jesus visited me," said Pastor Tson, "and made me ready for the battle again."

Up from the Grave We Arose

My Dear Shepherds,

A man, dead to rights, three days buried, walked into the city of the dead and said, "Repent!" Revival—resurrection—broke out. That's "the sign of Jonah" (Luke 11:29-30). Jesus fulfilled that sign, and now, so do we who represent his gospel message. The preaching part isn't nearly so hard as our death in the belly of the beast.

Did anyone prepare you in seminary for the routine rigor of dying? Even when we occasionally heard that pastoring would be hard I don't think we got the message that it was lethal. And repetitive! Jesus said that all his followers must take up their cross. All Christians must engage in dying when we walk with Jesus. But I think ministry leaders, if their souls are sensitive, are subject to more dying, deeper dying, than many others. Paul spoke for our company when he wrote,

> We always carry around in our body the death of Jesus, so that the life of Jesus may also be revealed in our body. For we who are alive are always being given over to death for Jesus' sake, so that his life may also be revealed in our mortal body. So then, death is at work in us, but life is at work in you. (2 Cor. 4:10-12)

Recently, some of God's people have been especially cruel to their shepherds. Some shepherds have watched their sheep leave. Some of you grew so weary or discouraged that you felt like your own gravedigger. Perhaps some of you have looked into your souls and seen a dangerous virus breeding there. Or maybe you just saw emptiness.

A pastor told me that for the first ten years of his ministry life he was afflicted with a crippling anxiety disorder. The seed of some small worry would erupt virulently into sickening panic. His wife would make him read the Bible aloud while he paced back and forth in their small bedroom until he calmed down. He said that 2 Corinthians 4:16-18 became his lifeline. There, after Paul affirmed his hope of resurrection for him and the Corinthians, he said,

> *Therefore we do not lose heart. Though outwardly we are wasting away, yet inwardly we are being renewed day by day. For our light and momentary troubles are achieving for us an eternal glory that far outweighs them all. So we fix our eyes not on what is seen, but on what is unseen, since what is seen is temporary, but what is unseen is eternal.*

My pastor friend said, "I prayed many years, 'Lord, take this away from me.' The way the Lord answered was to tell me that this suffering was temporary and fleeting. He gave me an eternal perspective to see the day when all things would be made right." There was a second takeaway for him. "That text rebuked me," he said, "for thinking on all the things that could go wrong. My anxiety was coming from fleeting things when the text was telling me to take heart in the things that are eternal." By God's grace, he is much healthier now and his ministry has the vitality of a dead man resurrected.

Paul said, "We are being *renewed* day by day." The word means "qualitatively new," a new beginning, re-creation. That is true whether I awake feeling like a new man or not. What's more, these troubles—this daily dying—re-creates us little by little into the image of Christ, which will only be fully evident when heaven reveals in us "an eternal weight of glory beyond all comparison."

He Lingered

My Dear Shepherds,

Why did he linger? Jesus had endured the worst of the world. He had slept in its stables and faced its beasts. He had borne its insults and faithlessness. He had tasted its tears and vinegar. He had cringed under its whips and thorns, and agonized under its spikes and sins. He descended to the deepest place a soul can go, to a dungeon which no key had ever unlocked. So, when he had wrenched the heavy doors of death from their hinges and walked free why did he linger in the graveyard? Even the most breathtaking spring dawn has about it the pall of death compared to the fragrances and breezes of heaven.

Why did he linger when all heaven waited to welcome him? With the chance to bound from the pit of impenetrable darkness to the glory of ineffable light, from the screams of demons to the songs of the angels, from the agony of death to the ecstasy of glory, why did he linger? When all of heaven waited to welcome him home, when a new song waited to be sung, when the throne awaited its king, and the crowns their sole sovereign, why would he linger to be mistaken for a gardener at the grave? Why return for Thomas' skeptical examination? Why stroll unrecognized with the grief-stricken disciples? Why did he linger?

Upon the Cross, Christ had cried with his dying breath, "It is finished." Salvation was secured. Death defeated. The Holy Spirit ready for his Pentecostal arrival. It seemed as though there were no loose ends left, no details unattended, no work undone. So why would he linger?

He lingered for love's sake, of course, to convince his followers—more than 500 eyewitnesses—that he was indeed alive. Not just resuscitated either, but a new Adam, fashioned not from dust but the firstborn from among the dead. When he breathed on his disciples and said, "Receive the Holy Spirit," he gave them their first inkling that they would no longer be what they had been. Ever since, faith in Christ vitalizes us with the breath of his life, day in and day out, now and forever.

Dying would come, too. Jesus' followers all carry crosses. We all die daily. That is especially and painfully true for those who shepherd the Lord's flocks. The work has been discouraging, the Lord's people—some of them—worse than unkind. A lot of pastors are gasping these days. Many are breathless. In order to persevere we must breathe deeply of the risen Christ, inhaling his Holy Spirit. Otherwise, we will suffer spiritual emphysema. Paul, who knew about ministry mortality, tells us his remedy:

> So we fix our eyes not on what is seen, but on what is unseen, since what is seen is temporary, but what is unseen is eternal. (2 Cor. 4:18)

A young pastor who I respect deeply told me, "Even when people were cruel to me I wanted to die for them. I bear the weight of a thousand stories no one else can know. And as I do, I feel from somewhere deep within me a glimmer of hope, that just as it was for Jesus, after the weight of suffering comes a place without tears and a crown for the one who suffers well." He added, "You have to think about this stuff. Either that or I'll quit, and I can't do that."

Jesus lingers for you, willing to share your sufferings so that you might inhale his life.

God Plays Favorites

My Dear Shepherds,

Jacob is the Bible's "Everyman." He is the first Israel. (Jesus is the second.) Jacob embodied the nation of Israel, literally and figuratively. And he is us. Not at our best, certainly, and not so much once Christ gets hold of us, but we are all Jacobs—grasping for blessings we don't fully believe, glimpsing the glory of Yahweh, disappointed by our Labans and Leahs, but always in the grip of God.

You may not have read Jacob's story in a long while. Most pastors have never preached on him. But I found my fourteen sermons on his life, stretching from Genesis 25 through 35, plus 48, to be among the most fascinating series of my career. After 20 years exiled to the household of his greasy uncle and father-in-law (twice over), Laban, God summoned Jacob to return to the land and life promised him. When Laban chased him down the LORD protected him and then, when Jacob "went on his way, the angels of God met him." Not until the shepherds outside Bethlehem did anyone see so many angels as Jacob! Yet Jacob was "in great fear and distress" because Esau was coming to meet him with 400 men.

He prayed well, to our surprise; the best prayer in Genesis, in fact. The heart of his prayer is familiar to us all: "O God ... save me, I pray ..." (Gen. 32:9-12). We all know that prayer by heart! It is a prayer standard, especially for pastors. Pastoring isn't safe work. I was so often afraid—afraid of brewing conflicts, critics, not performing adequately, that my weak prayers left us defenseless, that I would be our church's undoing. Fear is often the front door to the school of prayer.

Most of the threats Jacob faced were of his own making. He deserved Esau's wrath and Laban's conniving. We don't deserve all that we fear but that is small comfort. But when we're afraid, trust this: God plays favorites. When God plays favorites we call it grace. And you, dear shepherd, are among his favorites.

Despite God's earlier promises, Jacob couldn't imagine that God would actually treat him as his favored son. Pastors are prone to that same assumption. I used to think that Jesus was pointing straight at my ministry when he said, "From everyone who has been given much, much will be demanded," and "When you have done everything you were told to do, you should say, 'We are unworthy servants; we have only done our duty." So it was no wonder that I was often afraid, that I so often felt I'd have to face and fight my own battles. It went with the job.

But, dear shepherds, the angels of God are with us! Psalm 91 promises, "For he will command his angels concerned you to guard you in all your ways." By the end of this story, Jacob could raise his hand to give witness, "Even when you deserve the worst, God will not treat you as your sins deserve. Instead he will treat you as his favorite!"

In his wonderful book, *Gentle and Lowly*, Dane Ortlund writes, "Jesus is not trigger-happy. Not harsh, reactionary, easily exasperated. He is the most understanding person in the universe. The posture most natural to him is not a pointed finger but open arms."

That said, there is a danger we all face. Not the army of Esau but the ambush of God.

'The Magnificent Defeat'

My Dear Shepherds,

"So Jacob was left alone and a man wrestled with him" (Gen. 32:24). Oh, make no mistake, he was no mere man. By the end of that dark night Jacob whispered, "I saw *God* face to face, and yet my life was spared."

After 20 years of exile, Jacob was finally returning to the land God had promised him, but before he could get there he had to face his twin brother, Esau, whom he had cheated out of both birthright and blessing all those years ago. And while Esau was coming with an army of 400 men, little did Jacob know that the real threat ahead of him was not his brother but God himself. Read the account in Genesis 32:24-32.

Verse 25 says, "When the man saw that he could not overpower him . . . ." How could that be? Jacob was strong, but he wasn't *that* strong. But then again, this wasn't a mere matter of muscle. It was a contest of wills, and Jacob's will was herculean, very nearly a match for God! Yet as the old African American preachers used to say, "Your arm's too short to box with God."

One reason I regard Jacob as the Bible's Everyman is that all those whom God loves will find themselves, at one time or another, ambushed by Yahweh, whom Jacob called the "Fear of Isaac" (Gen. 31:42, 53). At certain times, between us and the life God has promised, lurks "the beloved Enemy" bent on our "magnificent defeat," to use Frederick Buechner's phrases.

Pastoring is hard work. Really hard work. The pandemic has made it insufferable for many pastors. I have an email before me from a pastoral couple who wrote, "We are seriously wondering how much longer we can do this, but God has not released us." Jacob nods ruefully and says, "I know the feeling." It may feel like your struggles are with your people, but don't be too sure. God is good at disguises.

So when "the man" couldn't overpower Jacob, he crippled him. God doesn't really fight fair, as we all learn. I assume that at first Jacob tried to escape the man who ambushed him but sometime during those dark, sweat-stained hours, Jacob realized he had God within his grasp and if he let go he might never get him back. Hosea 12:4 says that Jacob "wept and begged for his favor." Jacob gasped, "I will not let you go unless you bless me."

I know, as you do, what it is to be wrestled to my knees by God. In my young years, having never failed at anything in my life, I was let go from my first two ministry jobs. Again and again I prayed, "Lord, please let me do something that will matter in a hundred years." It was my version of praying for God's favor. Another time, years later, I had to publicly ask forgiveness for responding too harshly to some people in a congregational meeting. It was hard enough to get up in front of the congregation, but what was really hard was to mean it. That was a long, dark struggle between God and me. There have been a few other matches, each which God won. I never thought to pray in those times, "I will not let you go unless you bless me," but neither did I let go of God.

That, dear brothers and sisters, is how God wrestles with us and, paradoxically, how we overcome him. There we lie, like Jacob, in the mud and blood, clinging to God when he says, "You win. I will bless you."

The Blessed Limp

My Dear Shepherds,

Ever since I staggered through a sermon early in my career on Jacob wrestling with the man/angel/God in Genesis 32:22-32, I've been drawn to this mysterious, profound story. One of the vexing puzzles was this: The whole struggle came down to Jacob weeping and begging (Hos. 12:3-4), "I will not let you go until you bless me," so I'd expect to hear a blessing, but it seems like we never do.

This is not a one-off story. It is archetypal, repeated in the lives of all those blessed by God. In the upside-down world of his grace, God *surrenders* his blessing only to those whom he *defeats*. His blessing for Jacob and for us has three parts.

"When the man saw that he could not overpower him, he touched the socket of Jacob's hip," crippling him. There's the first blessing: the limp. Verse 32 says that ever after the Israelites were not to eat that tendon (sort of like the way we save the wishbone) so they would not forget the painful way God blesses his people.

Jacob's dislocated hip reminds us that God will do what he must to bring us to our knees before him. This happens to every believer, perhaps not because of sin, but always to bless us. C. S. Lewis wrote, "We are not necessarily doubting that God will do the best for us; we are wondering how painful the best will turn out to be." Famously, it happened to Paul. He described his "thorn in the flesh" in 2 Corinthians 12:7-10 and how God told him, "My grace is sufficient for you, for my power is made perfect in weakness."

Ministry life comes with crippling times because, like Paul, we must not only experience the value of weakness for ourselves but become living evidence of God's strength for those we shepherd. Our failures, inabilities, heartbreaks, sicknesses, griefs, even our besetting sins—all these "messengers of Satan," whispering and wheedling their words of defeat—have been the hip-wrenching, merciful work of God to bring us low, to make our souls child-sized.

Every Christian biography that's been written, told, or only held silently in our hearts—every single one—has a chapter telling the story of the blessed limp. In his autobiography, *Love Hunger*, my friend and classmate, David Kyle Foster, wrote how after an amazing saving by Christ and a superb theological education, he could find no place to minister. He writes,

> One night, I poured out my heart to God, telling him that I could not take it anymore. Since he had placed this powerful call on my life, he needed to give it an outlet or just take me home. My heart was weighed down with heaviness, as if an elephant were sitting on it. I cried out, "Lord, I'm literally dying inside." In his still, small voice, he gently replied, "That's what's supposed to be happening." As soon as he said it, I knew that it was not only true—it was wonderfully true. As if I were looking in a mirror for the first time, I saw that I was full of myself—my ardor, my training, my need to be affirmed. Yes, I needed to die. Otherwise, my service for the Kingdom would be polluted with self rather than being a selfless overflowing of my love for him.[1]

Undoubtedly, some who read this right now groan over the wrenching pain God has inflicted upon you. You will never again walk without that God-given limp. None of us do. But that limp will be your boast and blessing when day breaks.

---

[1]David Kyle Foster, *Love Hunger: A Harrowing Journey from Sexual Addition to True Fulfillment* (Grand Rapids: Baker Publishing, 2014), p. 263.

Your Name Will Be God-Wrestler

My Dear Shepherds,

The turning point of his life started like this: "So Jacob was left alone, and a man wrestled with him till daybreak" (Gen. 32:22-32). In the end, Jacob, Heel-grabber, brought low and crippled, hung on for dear life to the heel of God himself. "I will not let you go unless you bless me," he sobbed. The mysterious man's reply added insult to injury. "What is your name?" he asked. "Jacob," he replied, like someone saying, "Guilty, your honor." (The last time he'd been asked that, by his aged, blind father, Isaac, he'd lied and said his name was Esau.)

The great irony of this story is that during his life Jacob had been blessed, re-blessed, and divinely reassured not once but twice, not to mention seeing God's favor over twenty years in both children and herds despite the conniving of his uncle, Laban. He knew God. He'd *seen* God. He heard God's promises. He saw God's favor. He met God's angels. And he prayed his heart out. But he just didn't believe God's blessing could be his without a fight. So it was as if God said, "OK, if you won't receive this great, free gift package I want to give you, I'll wrestle you for it." Because that was the only language Jacob seemed to understand.

In the sport of wrestling there is a move called a reversal, when the guy on the bottom suddenly pulls a move that puts him on top. That is what Jacob pulled off that night. Hosea 12:4 says of Jacob, "He struggled with the angel and overcame him;" (and here comes his reversal) "he wept and begged for his favor." Jacob *overcame* his divine opponent?! By weeping and begging for his favor? That, my friends, is the only way to wrestle successfully with the Almighty. God falls for it every time.

"Then the Man said, 'Your name will no longer be Jacob, but Israel, because you have struggled with God and with humans and have overcome.'" Jacob got three bonus blessings: his limp, his new name, and his glimpse of God's face. His name, Israel, is captured by *The*

Message as "God-Wrestler." Frankly, I think I'd rather just be named Champ and skip the bout.

Alexander Maclaren wrote, "That name [Israel] was transmitted to his descendants, and has passed over to the company of believing men [and women], who have become overcome by God and prevailed with God. It is a charter and a promise. It is a stringent reminder of duty and a lofty ideal. A true Christian is an 'Israel.' His office is to wrestle with God."

All who serve the LORD will wrestle with him sooner or later. Even Jesus. It seems that at certain times the God-blessed life requires a heartbreaking struggle with the Lord. He may require us to face our resentments and disappointments over the Labans and Leahs, the long, lean years, or our lurking Esau-fears. Perhaps it's the deep disappointment that we never really got the life or ministry we hoped we had coming to us. We may have to face sins or follies we've ignored. In the mercy of God, we might realize that the good we strived for all these years was a free gift of grace that was ours for the taking all along, thanks to Jesus. God doesn't defeat us so much as he finally makes us willing to surrender to his mercy.

Our unseen contests with God mark us; they give us a new identity, as they did Jacob. We become Israels—humbled, limping, mercy-driven, blessed God-Wrestlers.

Seeing the Face of God

My Dear Shepherds,
Why does Jacob beg God for his blessing that dark night of wrestling when God had given him his great and timeless blessing twenty years before—the promise of the land, of a vast nation, and this:

> *All peoples on earth will be blessed through you and your off-spring. I am with you and will watch over you wherever you go, and I will bring you back to this land. I will not leave you until I have done what I have promised you.* (Gen. 28:14-15)

"What more can he say to you than he has already said?" The problem, I think, was that Jacob was not fit to carry such a promise. He didn't have the quality of faith necessary to carry it.

Pastors are emissaries of Christ, the great fulfilled Promise of God, but we are not made adequate to the task by our education, experience, nor even our calling. Our message depends on our faith, and the means God used to make Jacob a man of faith (albeit a weakling in it), are the means he uses with us.

"Then the man said, 'Let me go, for it is daybreak.'" But Jacob, hanging on for dear life, gasped, "I will not let you go unless you bless me." I suspect the Wrestler smiled. Then, finally ... *finally*, "God blessed him there," which I assume means that God reiterated his promise of 20 years before.

> *So Jacob called the place Peniel [Face of God], saying, "It is because I saw God face to face, and yet my life was spared." The sun rose above him as he passed Peniel, and he was limping because of his hip.* (Gen. 32:31-32)

That's not only a fact, it is pure poetry. Apparently the dawn gave Jacob a glimpse of the divine Wrestler and what he saw was like seeing the rising sun shining on him!

We all know the heavy shadows that come sometimes with "these people you have given me," (to quote Moses), the disappointments, criticisms, and self-doubt that so often eclipse the bright face of God. Return to Peniel, "the light of the knowledge of God's glory displayed in the face of Christ" (2 Cor. 4:6).

Ever since Aaron, our God-given birthright has been spoken over us, including the words, "The Lord make his face shine upon you." It is a beaming image, like a mother seeing her infant walk or a father seeing his prodigal while he is still a long way off. So is our Father's beaming face when he looks upon us; when he sees you.

In his book, *The Wisdom of Tenderness*, Brennan Manning told this story, one of my favorites:

> Several years ago, Edward Farrell of Detroit took his two-week vacation to Ireland to celebrate his favorite uncle's eightieth birthday. On the morning of the great day, Ed and his uncle got up before dawn, dressed in silence, and went for a walk along the shores of Lake Killarney. Just as the sun rose, his uncle turned and stared straight at the rising orb. Ed stood beside him for twenty minutes with not a single word exchanged. Then the elderly uncle began to skip along the shoreline, a radiant smile on his face.
>
> After catching up with him, Ed commented, "Uncle Seamus, you look very happy. Do you want to tell me why?"
>
> "Yes, lad," the old man said, tears washing down his face. "You see, the Father is fond of me. Ah, me Father is so very fond of me".[1]

[1]Brennan Manning, *The Wisdom of Tenderness* (San Francisco: Harper One, 2004), pp. 25-26.

Surprise Ending

My Dear Shepherds,

Jacob never imagined the ending. Grace is like that.

Peniel—"Face of God," Jacob's wrestling place at the River Jabbok, lay behind him. The sun, which at dawn had caught the gleam of God's face, now stood high and hot. In the distance four hundred fighting men raised a dark cloud of dust. At their head stood Esau, a bear of a man with wild red hair and beard.

For twenty years Jacob had been the ill-equipped, mostly faithless, bearer of God's great Abrahamic blessing. Then, during the grueling night that had just passed, God faith-fitted him with a humbled limp, a new identity—Israel (God-Wrestler), and a life-changing glimpse of God's bright face. But no sooner did Jacob leave one foe than he faced another. Esau approached with a menacing army and a festering grudge. Jacob situated his wives and sons with his favorites farthest from danger. Then "he himself went on ahead and bowed down to the ground seven times as he approached his brother" (Gen. 33:3).

What happens next is a stunner—the surprise ending that, if you didn't already know it, would leave you teary and sniffling. "But Esau ran to meet Jacob and embraced him; he threw his arms around his neck and kissed him. And they wept" (v. 4). Nobody but God saw *that* coming!

Do those words ring a bell? "But while he was still a long way off, his father saw him and was filled with compassion for him; he ran to his son, threw his arms around him and kissed him" (Luke 15:20). Kenneth E. Bailey opened my eyes to this in *Jacob & the Prodigal: How Jesus Retold Israel's Story*. It's hard to imagine two characters more different than Esau and the father in Jesus' story but they had this in common: neither had any reason to welcome their respective prodigals, each who had broken faith with them, yet each portrays the face of God's grace.

That's what Jacob said: *"For to see your face is like seeing the face of*

God, now that you have received me favorably" (v. 10). Only hours before, Jacob had actually *seen* God's face and been spared [saved] (Gen. 32:30), so this was no mere flattery. It was a theological *Aha!* moment. Jacob was saved by grace twice in one day.

Most pastors are limping these days; a beleaguered company of Israels in a long season of God-wrestling. So many shepherds ache over flocks who bicker about masks, politics, or over sheep who seemed to have slipped away from the flock under cover of Covid. Under the cloud of all this disappointment it is easy to project that God must be disappointed with you, too, or that your own unmet expectations mirror his. But you are called and outfitted to carry his Blessing, Jesus Christ. You come bowing over and over in apprehension but God in his grace runs to meet those whom he has prepared to carry his promise in Christ. He runs to meet you, not because you are a prodigal but because you are a weary shepherd of his beloved sheep and a bearer of his blessing.

After their grace-kissed reunion, Jacob and Esau parted and Jacob finally went home to Shechem. "There he set up an altar and called it El Elohe Israel," which means, Mighty Is the God of the God-Wrestler (Gen. 33:20). There's a project for you, pastor. Leave your flock for a bit. Bow your head, heft altar stones into place, focus on the face of God's grace in Christ, and offer your sacrifices of thanksgiving to the mighty God of the God-Wrestler.

'You Know How I Lived'

My Dear Shepherds,

Before all this upheaval, pastors used to have at least some vague idea of whether or not we were being good shepherds. Now, in this season of social distancing, livestreaming, disinfecting, and Zoom meetings, who even knows?

Over the next few weeks let us get our bearings and our balance from Paul's farewell words to the Ephesian elders, a compass given to us in Acts 20. We'll take it slowly because these words are God's mercy to you, not another burden you are ill-equipped to carry.

> When they arrived, he said to them: "**You know how I lived** the whole time I was with you, from the first day I came into the province of Asia. **I served the Lord with great humility and with tears and in the midst of severe testing** by the plots of my Jewish opponents." (Acts 20:18-19)

Paul will talk about his Word work among them and the importance of shepherding their congregation but first he says this, "You know how I lived..." Ministry credibility starts here. Not with your vision, leadership, or study, but by how you live, in full view of your people, especially your leaders.

Paul shows us that serving the Lord requires three knee-benders that I suspect never appeared on any of our job descriptions.

"Great humility" comes to no one naturally. What's more, leading while holding a basin in one hand and a towel in the other can seem uncommonly difficult. Humility is not actually a virtue you can summon up by trying. Rather, it is awkward, personal truth-telling, taking off our clerical costume to reveal our rags and empty pockets. To put it another way (as Jesus did), humility is becoming child-sized so we can maneuver naturally through the low doors and narrow corridors of the kingdom.

Pastors, like Paul, also serve Jesus "with tears." Ministry brings a lot of moments that break our hearts, but Paul thought particularly of one burden. In verse 31 he said he "never stopped warning each of you night and day *with tears*." Pastors bear the weight of their people's destiny like parents anxiously waiting up for the kids to get home. I imagine that one of your burdens of these last months, distanced from your people as you've been, was worrying if they'd remain faithful, if they'd return stronger or weaker, or if they'd return at all. Who can blame you?

Finally, serving the Lord brought Paul "severe testing" from gospel enemies. Few of us face any opposition so severe as his but every pastor worth their salt has felt the diabolical pushback against kingdom progress. For a time, I led a seminary class where each week a student would bring a case study and we'd all talk through how to handle it. Those future pastors were analytical and theological but I realized they were missing something. "If you were in this situation," I began to ask, "what would it do to you? Given your personality and vulnerabilities, what kind of toll do you think it might take?"

Serving the Lord will take the stuffing out of any shepherd. Humility, heartbreak, and the inward toll of devilish trials are not only hard, but they need to be experienced in full view of your people. Pastors must keep plenty of secrets but our weaknesses aren't among them. Our flock doesn't need to know all our heartaches and failures but transparency and vulnerability under pressure are part of pastoring. Here is where we earn ministry credibility. These are the steep steps up to the pulpit. But there is a mercy in these things, too, for they free us from pretense. Our people are watching us, to be sure, but no longer up on that infernal pedestal.

Wordworkers

My Dear Shepherds,

I'm more of an Aaron than a Moses, a spokesman more than the leader. "Aaron told them everything the LORD had said to Moses." Like that.

Shepherds of God's flock are called to be Wordworkers. "Christ himself gave the apostles, the prophets, the evangelists, the pastors and teachers to equip God's people for works of service . . ." (Eph. 4:11-12). Each bring God's Word but with different voices, like a sacred choir singing gospel in four-part harmony.

When Paul said farewell to the Ephesian elders he began, "You know how I lived the whole time I was with you." His humble, tear-stained, battle-tested service gave Christlike credibility to his Wordwork.

> *You know that I have not hesitated to **preach** anything that would be helpful to you but have **taught** you publicly and from house to house. I have **declared** to both Jews and Greeks that they must turn to God in repentance and have faith in our Lord Jesus.* (Acts 20:20-21)

I'm sure Paul had other tasks to do, like all pastors, but none of those defined his ministry. **What matters most in our ministries is delivering God's Word to both believers and unbelievers.** All good shepherds have a Spirit-given instinct, affinity, and capacity for Scripture. After all, a shepherd who cannot handle the Bible is like a shepherd without rod and staff, helpless to feed, lead, or guard the flock.

We don't go about our work merely spouting Bible verses. Our Wordwork requires us to target from the Bible, "anything that would be helpful," as we are led by the Spirit.

I asked an elder of a rural church, who asked me to fill their pulpit, what their church needs. "Our pastor has left and we're worried about declining population. How do we lead now?" So with that need in mind,

I must pray, listen, push into my Bible, and think. Then I will know how to bring God's Word to them.

Remember: everything in Scripture is counterintuitive. None of it comes naturally to us or to our people. All of it, every word, is God-breathed. And all of it spells out what was once only unimaginable mystery, that "grace and truth came through Christ Jesus" and "Christ in you [is] the hope of glory."

So at every pastoral turn we must be ready to declare "anything that would be helpful to you," sometimes teaching, other times rebuking or correcting, or basic training in righteousness, but always "so that the servant of God may be thoroughly equipped for every good work" (2 Tim. 3:16-17).

I know you face incredible pressures, distractions, and duties, but **nothing pastors do matters more than our Wordwork.** We enter people's lives, like heralds with long brass trumpets, like physicians carrying scalpel and ointment, like nursing mothers and watchful fathers, like sowers with seeds, and sentinels with sword at the ready.

We declare the plain gospel: repent and believe in the Lord Jesus. We bring Scripture's assurance of mercy for those whose sins are burdensome and toxic. We open our Bibles to quiet fears and to instill God-given hope. With the rod and staff of Scripture we walk people away from the tempter and the pit, meet prodigals far from home, introduce brothers and sisters to life in God's household, direct the distracted to see the chariots of fire guarding us, and the path of righteousness illumined by the lamp of God's Word. We deliver God's covenants, the lyrics for our praises and laments, the stern summons of the prophets, the astonishing stories of witnesses to the past and the future, and the love letters of the Bridegroom. All because God gifted us to his church as Wordworkers.

To Finish

My Dear Shepherds,

Six or seven years into pastoral life I became deeply fatalistic about my future. I saw other pastors, some dear to me, fail and were forced to leave the ministry. I was frightened. I thought, *I'm no better than they are. If it happened to them, it will happen to me. It's just a matter of time.*

I thought often of Pickett's Charge at the Battle of Gettysburg when 15,000 Confederate troops marched into the entrenched guns of the Union Army and were decimated, suffering 6,000 casualties! Some went down early while others almost took the hill, but in the end they all fell or retreated. I pictured ministry—*my* ministry—as that ill-fated.

Then, in the great mercy of God, I found Jude 24, "To him who is able to keep you from stumbling and to present you before his glorious presence without fault and with great joy . . ." I threw my arms around that promise like a drowning man seizing a life preserver.

Now, decades later, and recently retired from our church, I breathe easier. Not because I'm particularly stronger but because I'm familiar with the grip of God's grace, his hand on my back, and his insistent voice, "This is the way; walk in it."

In Paul's farewell to the Ephesian elders, he told them that the Holy Spirit had made clear that the way ahead for him led to "prison and hardships." Then Paul said,

> *However, I consider my life worth nothing to me; my only aim is to finish the race and complete the task the Lord Jesus has given me—the task of testifying to the good news of God's grace.*
> (Acts 20:24)

Once, and only once, I ran a 5K to raise money for a friend's missions trip. It was a very hot, muggy afternoon and before I was even half finished I literally feared that my heart couldn't take it. But I'd raised a lot of pledges with the promise that I would not stop. So I didn't. It wasn't pretty but I finished. Pastoring has been like that sometimes. There have been times when I wanted to do anything else—sell shoes or be a Walmart greeter, *anything*! But I'd promised to run the race and complete the task.

I don't think pastors fail because the burdens are too heavy or the enemies too fierce. I wonder if the difference between finishing and failing—the one test that is up to us—is simply *being true*. The silent, secret pressure upon pastors, in ways no other Christians face, is to fake it. To put on our preacher voice, our shepherd's bathrobe costume, to let prayers roll off our tongues having never passed through our souls, and to preach sermons we ourselves haven't heard. We don't have to be legalistic Pharisees to slowly become hypocrites.

To run the race, we must, of course, keep our eyes on the finish line. We must remember what we're called to do: "testifying to the good news of God's grace." But we cannot convey the gospel authentically when we no longer take the measure of our own souls and when we've lost our own way to God's throne of grace.

I remember watching a play where the actor picked up a suitcase. He leaned into it a little but I knew—we all knew—that suitcase was really empty. He couldn't fake the weight of it. So it is with the ministry. None of us will finish well if we've taken up acting.

But what could be more heartening for pastors than to know that the Lord Jesus is able to keep us from falling away from him and from our calling. This is not Pickett's Charge. To be sure, we must be brave and we must soldier on. But more than anything else, *we must be true*. We cannot play make-believe. Run to Jesus. The LORD, high and holy, always welcomes and revives "the one who is contrite and lowly in spirit." Run to Jesus and "find rest for your souls."

'Testifying to the Good News of God's Grace'

My Dear Shepherds,

Doctors enter the practice of medicine. Lawyers, the practice of law. Pastors enter the practice of grace. Grace is our stock-in-trade. But practicing grace is not much like the professions of medicine or law.

Paul summed up his ministry goal when he bid farewell to the Ephesian elders: "my only aim is to finish the race and complete the task the Lord Jesus has given me—*the task of testifying to the good news of God's grace*" (Acts 20:24). Evangelical Wordworkers know that we must always declare *and* embody God's grace in Christ.

But there are ways even the most committed gospel preachers hinder their gospel work. Did you ever inadvertently try to drive without releasing the emergency brake on your car? You can go but something's not right. There's a drag.

Our declaration of God's grace drags when we grow lax about mining treasures, old and new, from Scripture. Grace, like manna, must be collected afresh every morning. Preachers can default to the familiar, thinking that's all they have, or that it will do. It's also possible to study and preach a text thoroughly yet leave the good news of God's grace gasping for life because we dissected it instead of awakening it.

Every sermon or lesson is like the lifeless Adam until God breathes into it the breath of life. Sometimes that breath came for me in a moment deep in study when a jewel I'd never seen peeked out from the print. Other times prayer laid bare a wound, deficit, or ignorance within me and God's grace in my text came like Jesus himself to heal, fill, or enlighten me. But I warn you: never preach without that breath of grace.

Another inadvertent drag is captured by a pastor friend who wrote to me, "I can feel like I'm not worthy to be a pastor. I can give others grace but have a hard time giving it to myself." That is a familiar occupational hazard. I often found myself weighed and wanting by Jesus' words regarding "the faithful and wise manager": "From everyone who has been given much, much will be demanded; and from the one who has been entrusted with much, much more will be asked" (Luke 12:48). Taken out of context, as I always did, there was no room there for pastoral grace. No rest for the weary. At my best I'd only be doing my job, and anything less than my constant best was unacceptable.

But that kind of servitude muffles the preaching of grace, like trying to communicate while wearing our surgical masks. Our preaching may be no less true or gracious but it's weakened like a boxer pulling his punches or like a trumpet player who always uses a mute.

In his remarkable book, *Gentle and Lowly: The Heart of Christ for Sinners and Sufferers,* Dane Ortlund writes, "Only as we drink down the kindness of the heart of Christ will we leave in our wake, everywhere we go, the aroma of heaven, and die one day having startled the world with glimpses of a divine kindness too great to be boxed in by what we deserve." That goes for pastors. In fact, it is essential for pastors.

Pastoral work is hard and draining. The blessed counterbalance to the wearisome weight of ministry is "the task of testifying to the good news of God's grace." That's what can keep us putting one foot in front of the other. Dispensing and embodying God's grace in Christ is like spiritual adrenaline energizing a weary runner.

We are divinely authorized to testify to the good news of God's grace in every sermon, counseling session, discipleship meeting, hospital call, wedding, and funeral. We pull on its red thread in every Scripture text we preach. We bury our sins in the sea of God's forgetfulness. We boldly plant our prayers and our future on the high ground of God's grace in Christ. And when we wonder if we will finish well we remember, "grace has led me safe thus far, and grace will lead me home."

'It's a Thing of the Soul'

My Dear Shepherds,

Dr. Tim Laniak, an Old Testament professor at Gordon-Conwell Seminary, Charlotte, interviewed a Bedouin shepherd in Jordan.

> *Q. How many sheep and goats do you have?*
> A. 2000. I have the biggest flock in this area . . .
> *Q. How many did you start with?*
> A. I began with one in 1984. And I still know every one of them. They are like family to me.
> *Q. With that many, you still know every one of them?*
> A. Yes. I am with the flocks every day. Although I have homes in the village, I stay out here with them during the summer [migration]. I must personally supervise the care of the sheep or I shouldn't be a shepherd . . . *It's a thing of the soul; it's not a business.*

As Paul bid a tearful farewell to the elders of the Ephesian church, he took them back again to their calling:

> *Keep watch over yourselves and all the flock of which the Holy Spirit has made you overseers.* Be shepherds of the church of God, *which he bought with his own blood.* (Acts 20:28)

There are three easy-to-pass phrases there which get to the soul of shepherds.

"Keep watch *over yourselves.*" We are shepherds of ourselves as well as our congregation. Pastors face a unique challenge to be *true*, authentic, and genuine before Christ and others. I met a pastor recently who told me about a small group he was in some 15 years ago. Of the six couples in the group, four were in ministry in a large evangelical church. Of those four, two are in the process of divorce and a third is out of the ministry. One of the lay couples is also divorced. Only one pastoral couple remains strong. He wrote, "The unrecognized vulnerability, I believe, was blindness to and lack of honesty about true struggles/brokenness and an unwillingness to enter deep discipleship, healing, and self-care with Jesus." *That's* why we must pay careful attention to ourselves.

"The flock of which *the Holy Spirit has made you overseers.*" The Holy Spirit laid a cape of calling on you. You are not your own ever again. Christ captured us once in salvation and then again in giving us to the upward bound procession of his glad servants. But he did not leave us to our own devices. The Holy Spirit gives us the instincts and the company of the Good Shepherd. The Spirit also gives us the Lord's own imprimatur, carrying his endorsement of us to our people. Incredibly they see us as God's own emissaries.

"The church of God, *which he bought with his own blood.*" Our sheep are often so ordinary. Some are so consistently contrary. Others are careless of their own souls, bewildered by life, or prone to wander. Most will much sooner attend a potluck than a prayer meeting. But the Lord bought them with his own blood.

God gathered them in one place and assigned them to us, to feed them the whole will of God, to attend to the young, to herd them toward pasture and guard them from predators, to bring them to the Lord's own bath and table, to walk with them and Jesus into death's valley and watch as they step over the threshold into the house of the Lord forever.

"I must personally supervise the care of the sheep or I shouldn't be a shepherd," the Bedouin shepherd said. "It's a thing of the soul; it's not a business." So oversee your own soul. Be confident in your cape, the mantle that the Spirit has draped over your shoulders. And do not forget that those ordinary people you shepherd, including yourself, were redeemed by the blood of Jesus our Lord.

Guardians

My Dear Shepherds,

Each Sunday before service a few of us gathered to pray. I would always pray about visitors, and that God would keep the wolves away from our door.

When Paul bid farewell to the Ephesian elders, knowing he'd never see them again, he warned them,

> *I know that after I leave, savage wolves will come in among you and will not spare the flock. Even from your own number men will arise and distort the truth in order to draw away disciples after them. So be on your guard! Remember that for three years I never stopped warning each of you night and day with tears.*
> (Acts 20:29-31)

The prospect of savage wolves circling my flock just beyond my sight or perhaps right under my nose unnerved me, like hearing a footfall somewhere in our house at 3 a.m.

We all know difficult and dangerous troublemakers in our congregations but wolves are rare. As Paul intimates, they tend to emerge from church leadership—pastors, elders, or teachers—people positioned to lead others astray. You or I could become our own worst enemy.

Wolves aren't merely contrary or critical people. Wolves "distort the truth in order to draw away disciples after them." One pastor told me of a colleague who began teaching something akin to purgatory and, when challenged, left with his new little flock. He eventually descended to teaching polygamy, at which point even the gullible left! Wolfish shepherds lead people to barren boondocks and dry creek beds.

Wolves take a gospel truth, twist it from its orthodox ligaments, choke off the life-breath of the Spirit, and then proclaim it with diabolical effect. Flannery O'Conner was on to this folly when she wrote in her novel, *Wise Blood*, about a charlatan who renamed himself Onnie Jay Holy and had the audacity to form the "Holy Church of Christ Without Christ." Wolves distort Christian virtues, smothering grace in legalism or untethering it from holiness with license until Jesus becomes unrecognizable.

I'm kind of a fraidy cat when I think about predators stalking my people. But pastors need to buck up and take our cues from David. Remember when he sought Saul's permission to go after Goliath? He said, "When a lion or a bear came and carried off a sheep from the flock, I went after it, struck it and rescued the sheep from its mouth.... The LORD who rescued me from the paw of the lion and paw of the bear will rescue me from the hand of this Philistine" (1 Sam. 17:35, 37). There's our model.

Do you wonder what happened to that church in Ephesus? When Jesus addressed them years later in Revelation 2:2, he said, "I know that you cannot tolerate wicked people, that you have tested those who claim to be apostles but are not, and have found them false." They had other faults but they had protected their flock from the wolves.

"For three years I never stopped warning each of you night and day with tears." He warned them of their own vulnerability. "If you think you are standing firm, be careful that you don't fall!" He drilled them in gospel doctrine. Handling the truth over and over gave them a feel for fakery. He instilled in them the life-and-death urgency of guarding the precious flock of God. The stakes had often brought him to tears.

Dr. Tim Laniak's interview with a Jordanian Bedoin shepherd concluded this way:

> Q.   *Have you ever lost any sheep?*
> A.   Yes, but I always looked for the ones that were lost until I found them–alive or dead. There is only one sheep that I couldn't find and it still bothers me every day.
> Q.   *How long would it take to teach me to be a good shepherd?*
> A.   Do you have the heart for it?

Safe

My Dear Shepherds,

Insecurity is an occupational hazard and a ministry inconsistency. We constantly assure our people of God's unwavering love and protection, yet it seems God so often pushes us to the breaking point of faith and confidence.

There's a story (true or not, I don't know) about Teresa of Avila, the tiny, feisty Spanish nun and mystic. She was making her way to her convent during a fierce rainstorm, then slipped down an embankment and fell squarely into the mud. The irrepressible nun looked up to heaven and admonished her Maker, "If this is how You treat Your friends, no wonder You have so few of them!" We all know the feeling.

Imagine what the Ephesian elders felt when Paul bid them farewell for the last time. He'd just warned them that "savage wolves" would arise to tear at their flock. Talk about unsettling! Then he gave them this assurance:

> *Now I commit you to God and the word of his grace, which can build you up and give you an inheritance among all those who are sanctified.* (Acts 20:32)

Paul wasn't conferring on them a new security they'd not had before. He was reassuring those shepherds—and us—that we are more prepared and able to guard the flock of God than we feel.

"I commit you to God," our ever present help in trouble. To God, who subverts the schemes of the evil one, turning them to our good. To God, who never sleeps, who always listens, and whose angels guard us in all our ways. To "the LORD, the LORD, the compassionate and gracious God, slow to anger, abounding in love and faithfulness." God is committed to us!

To be entrusted to God is security enough but added to that is "the word of his grace." We preach this gospel message, of course, but for believers that living Word gets into us, like breath into dry bones. It is a vaccine, an antidote, a transfusion. We are recreated, more miraculously by far than when God breathed life into first Adam. Never forget: we have been *born again*. Therein lies our safety and strength. We have within us, as breath itself, the Spirit of God, and "the mind governed by the Spirit is life and peace." We are *in* Christ, seated in the heavenly realms. We are impervious to the accusations of the devil, no matter how factual they may be. And we are immortal! "O death, where is your sting!"

How strong are good shepherds? God himself guards us and "the word of his grace" is in our blood.

Grace is the most God-blessed word in Scripture. Two specific "words of grace" have anchored my ministry. One, Luke 15:20, sometimes still brings tears to my eyes, "But while he was still a long way off, his father saw him and was filled with compassion for him; he ran to his son, threw his arms around him and kissed him." The other is the richest verse I know: "And God is able to bless you *abundantly* [make *all grace* abound to you], so that in *all* things at *all* times, having *all* that you need, you will *abound* in *every* good work" (2 Cor. 9:8).

Shepherding God's flock is daunting, to be sure, but we are stronger and abler than we feel, for God's "word of grace is able to build you up." That living grace, running through our veins, continues recreating us.

When I was about 35 my name was submitted for a significant leadership role. I gradually realized that I was embarrassed, not only because I lacked the necessary skills and temperament, but because I knew I did not have the character for such responsibility. I knew what others didn't, that I was too careless about sin, too irresponsible in my pursuit of godliness, too reliant on my talents. That was a quiet turning point. Now, decades later, I am better, smaller, because God's word of grace has indeed built me up. I am not alone in that. So it is for you, too.

Risk and Reward

My Dear Shepherds,

One time a large and wealthy church invited me to interview for a senior pastor role. My good friend attended the church so I called him and asked (facetiously), "If I was pastor there would I have a Mercedes in my driveway?" "Yes," he replied, "till the Elders left."

Pastors have always wryly observed that we didn't get into this for the money. Maybe money doesn't pose a temptation for you, but all of us are susceptible to covetousness—wanting what others have. Paul's last words to his beloved Ephesian elders were:

> *I have not coveted anyone's silver or gold or clothing. You yourselves know that these hands of mine have supplied my own needs and the needs of my companions. In everything I did, I showed you that by this kind of hard work we must help the weak, remembering the words the Lord Jesus himself said: "It is more blessed to give than to receive."* (Acts 20:33-35)

I think I was most prone to coveting other people's *ease*. I was usually grateful for my work and I certainly know others who worked much harder than I, so there was no excuse for the ease I coveted. But still there were times when I really wanted to be left alone like other people, or to have my evenings free like most folks, or, to go somewhere over the rainbow. My occasional discontent had many costumes.

As Paul exemplified to his elders, the antidote to coveting is not just to stop it but to *do* something: to help the weak at personal cost. Then the Lord Jesus' own clincher: "It is more blessed to give than receive." I wonder if we unconsciously assume he meant, "It is more *moral* to give than receive." Or, "You'll feel really great if you give rather than receive." I did not always feel great about giving to the weak. Occasionally I think I even resented it.

I remember a season, in the weeks after Easter, when I was just really tired of people. When I told the Lord I needed a break he said, "Would you do anything for me?" I replied, "Yes, Lord, you know I would." He said, "Would you even shine shoes for me?" (Strange, I know, but that's how it went.) "Yes, Lord, I'd even shine shoes." Then he whispered in my prayer, "Well, I don't really want you to shine shoes. But I do want you to spend time with some of my people." But in that, I was strangely refreshed.

Giving sacrificially to others draws God's blessing, which is never in mere equal measure to our service. In Acts 20:32, Paul assured us that God and the word of his grace would build us up "and give you *an inheritance* among all those who are sanctified." Our inheritance is our *reward* for serving Jesus (Col. 3:24). Jesus said, "The King will say to those on his right, 'Come, you who are blessed by my Father; *take your inheritance*, the kingdom prepared for you since the creation of the world. For I was hungry and you gave me something to eat, I was thirsty and you gave me something to drink, I was a stranger and you invited me in . . .'" (Matt. 25:34-35).

I can think of few Christians who have more opportunities to get rich slowly than pastors. When we trudge down hospital corridors or go back to the church for evening counseling, when we squeeze in a visit to a shut-in or meet with a 17-year-old just to talk about school, we are bringing food to hungry hearts. We are inviting in strangers. We are clothing people—maybe in garments of white. We go into prisons, some with unseen bars, and jingle the keys of grace. It is such ordinary service, so small, but look where it gets us: "in his glory, and all the angels with him."

"The King will reply, 'Truly I tell you, whatever you did for one of the least of these brothers and sisters of mine, you did for me.'"

'Sweet Sorrow'

My Dear Shepherds,

In these virus-corrupted, socially-distanced months several pastors I've known have concluded their ministries without proper farewells. Dave Ward's last Sunday was Easter, his last sermon to an empty auditorium. But he said he got an unexpected surprise parade of dozens of cars with church families. Another pastor friend, Susan Moody, grieved, "It feels like I am being robbed of some needed closure and celebration of what God has done through me. Celebrating that is really celebrating God and it strengthens me for the next task."

I thought of these colleagues when I came to the concluding description of Paul's farewell to the Ephesian elders:

> *When Paul had finished speaking, he knelt down with all of them and prayed. They all wept as they embraced him and kissed him. What grieved them most was his statement that they would never see his face again. Then they accompanied him to the ship.* (Acts 20:36-38)

In June, Pastor Jim Keena's last sermon, on this very text, was livestreamed to his church but with only a dozen folks in the auditorium. He told me, "I missed doing what Paul and the elders did in Acts 20:37. I missed weeping, embracing, and worshiping with the flock that God had entrusted to my care. I missed raising an Ebenezer and recalling God's past faithfulness and resting in God's future faithfulness."

In the early days of the shutdown, when our congregations could no longer meet, I thought a lot about the doctrine of the communion of the saints. I read Jesus' prayer in John 17, assuring our union with the Father through the Lord Jesus. Thus each of us, united with the triune God, are deeply and divinely united with one another. We often sense that the first time we meet a fellow Christian. So it stands to reason that partings would be more poignant and painful also.

Amidst all the noise and commotion of a commercial wharf, Paul "knelt down with all of them and prayed." What could be more natural than including God in a last huddle of Christian brothers? When I anticipated saying goodbye to my congregation of 22 years, I invited households to meet with me for prayer. Over the course of my last three weeks 55 of them came. Those were precious times.

I prayed with one couple for healing for a terrible family secret dumped upon them long ago. One brother brought me faded black-and-white pictures of his childhood home that he'd always meant to show me. One couple talked about God's healing of his cancer. One, a prayer warrior, asked me to pray for her wayward son. (More people asked me to pray about prodigal children than any other concern.) After I prayed with one of my elders and his wife we embraced and wept just as Paul had. I prayed with Connie, who died two months later of Covid-19. When I embraced and wept with one former leader he whispered, "We did some good work together," and I felt a great satisfaction. So it was for Paul and his elders there on that wharf.

It was Juliet who told Romeo, "Parting is such sweet sorrow that I shall say goodnight till be morrow." The prospect for Paul's elders of never seeing his face again came with the unspoken addition, "... never again *here*." That's the thing about Christian goodbyes. They sustain us till the morrow. Jim Keena said of his truncated farewell, "It makes me look forward to that Day when we'll give each other an eternal hello with never a bad goodbye."

Splendid Friends

My Dear Shepherds,

Herding sheep has never been a safe occupation, at least when it comes to the flock of God. Maybe I just never got the hang of the rod and staff but I've been plenty scared lots of times. For example, I came to our last church at a very scary time. There were simmering conflicts. People didn't trust each other. Most were disheartened. We were six weeks from bankruptcy. People were leaving. My very first Sunday I found myself having to arbitrate a looming split. I was so frightened. Then God brought Psalm 16 to me.

> *Keep me safe, my God,*
> *for in you I take refuge.*
> *I say to the LORD, "You are my Lord;*
> *apart from you I have no good thing."*

Pastors spend a lot of time helping God's people fend off fear but sometimes, when it is *our* fear, pursuing God's peace is a pretty lonely endeavor. In Psalm 16 David took his fear by the hand and marched into Israel's National Archives to review God's covenant with Israel. There, in God's ancient and timeless promises, his prayer for God's protection got a grip.

In those first weeks I specifically remember coming to verse 3:

> *I say of the holy people who are in the land,*
> *"They are the noble ones in whom is all my delight."*

I had already seen some disturbing behavior in my new congregation. Others were disillusioned and eyeing the door. I wondered what kind of people I had come to pastor. Then I read how David saw God's protection among God's saints, like God telling Elijah, "I reserve seven thousand in Israel—all whose knees have not bowed down to Baal."

There are holy people in this beleaguered congregation, I realized. Noble, splendid, high-born people of God who will help keep me safe and be the delight of my life. I wrote the date, 2/98, in the margin. Twenty-two years later when it came time to say goodbye I looked back on the safety and joy they'd brought me.

This psalm reminds us that we are not alone. We have precious brothers and sisters. *The Message* say it this way, "These God-chosen lives all around—what splendid friends they make!"

One night years ago I faced the wrath of a couple who felt I'd not adequately supported them. They'd asked to see me and insisted another elder and some friends be present also. The Lord pointed me to 1 Peter 2:23, "When they hurled their insults at him, he did not retaliate," so I bit my lip and kept quiet as they laid into me. But when they left I was black and blue. And, being a pastor, I had to go straight into another meeting as if nothing had happened.

It was about 9:30pm when everyone left. I was bone-tired and shaken. As I walked out of my office into the dark foyer I noticed a light on in the church library. I went to shut it off and found Tom there. "What are you doing here?" I asked. "I heard you had kind of a rough meeting," he said. "Yeah, it was," I agreed. Tears came to my eyes. When I regained my composure I asked, "Have you been waiting all this time? How did you know how long I'd be?" "I didn't," Tom said, "but I would have waited here all night to be sure you were alright." And he hugged me.

Yes, David, "what splendid friends they make!"

Our Feast and Estate

My Dear Shepherds,

When push comes to shove—which is exactly what happens in churches sometimes—pastors realize how insecure our positions are. Veteran pastors have this in common with the old gunslingers: we don't like to sit with our backs to the door. We know who's crouching there.

Our ministry risks and wounds should drive us to our knees and it is there that David hands us a prayer we need—Psalm 16.

> *Keep me safe, my God,*
> > *for in you I take refuge.*
> *I say to the LORD, "You are my Lord;*
> > *apart from you I have no good thing."*

Then David catalogs the good protections of God's covenant love, beginning with his "holy people." After that, we remember our untouchable inheritance.

> *LORD, you alone are my portion and my cup;*
> > *you make my lot secure.*
> *The boundary lines have fallen for me in pleasant places;*
> > *surely I have a delightful inheritance.* (Ps. 16:5-6)

Ministry impoverishes us in some ways. We go to bed hungry at heart. We begin to wonder who's hiding under our beds. That's why we pray—to reorient our souls and to check our investments.

In the LORD we live large. Christ feeds us a heaping portion of God! Our draught of destiny is Yahweh himself. It turns out that our estate is grander than our eyes can see. When we someday walk its perimeter we will be surprised how broad the boundaries were all along, how bright and beautiful the landscape that once seemed so hardscrabble.

As I stepped into my last year of pastoral work I had the uneasy feeling that I had grown too dispassionate about the Lord. I'd read of others who were aflame for Christ and I wasn't like that. I felt that perhaps God needed to take me to the woodshed for some stern words and correction.

Lent was approaching so I thought it would be the right season to take my medicine. I soberly decided I would endure a 36-hour fast each week, from Wednesday evening till Friday morning. I determined to set aside three hours on those Thursday mornings in order to listen to God and do a serious attitude check. That first Quiet Thursday I was unsure of just how to proceed so I got low and quiet before God and waited for the stern words I'd been expecting.

Without really realizing quite what was happening, I found myself watching scenes from my life, instances where God had taken care of me, disciplined me, taught me, blessed, and even honored me. I was caught up in those quickly passing scenes with no sense of time, watching my God-blessed life pass before my eyes. I could see Providence smiling even behind once-dark clouds. Then, as if my documentary was ending, these words concluded the presentation: "The boundary lines have fallen for me in pleasant places."

My Quiet Thursdays became precious. When the Father did talk soberly with me about some harbored sin, he was so kind and patient. I began to approach those hours as though entering my own Tent of Meeting where the very oxygen was God's love for me. The hunger of fasting simply embodied my yearning for God.

I usually sing benedictions at the end of worship services. One of my favorites is by Michael Card. In the first verse God promises, *"In this fearful, fallen place I will be your home,"* and in the second, *"From this fearful, fallen place I will bring you home."* Either way, the boundary lines have fallen for us in pleasant places!

Wonderful Counselor

My Dear Shepherds,

Some years ago one of my elders visited me. He came right out with it, "Lee, you're depressed and you're angry and you need to do something about it." So I summoned the courage to see a counselor where I came to realize that I lived in fear of what I thought of as *the mess*, the confounding and loaded situations I often had to face as a pastor. A simmering counseling situation, board tension, a lost sheep, a critic who must be faced, or just knowing that Euodia and Syntyche are at it again. *The mess.*

Pastors aren't neutral arbiters or consultants in the problems facing us. They suck us in. They affect our own souls. We need God's counsel, not only to help others but to guard our own hearts. David, a good shepherd, prayed for God's protection in Psalm 16: "Keep me safe, my God, for in you I take refuge." To bolster his faith, David then catalogued sources of God-given protection including this part of his prayer:

> *I will praise the Lord, who counsels me;*
> *even at night my heart instructs me.*
> *I keep my eyes always on the Lord.*
> *With him at my right hand, I will not be shaken.* (Ps. 16:7-8)

We might assume this means that I ask God what to do about a problem and then he tells me, but actually it doesn't always work like that, does it? The counselor I saw often just sat and waited, inviting me to surface what I was missing, to sort out and to own what to do or how to think. God the counselor does that, too. A lot of the time he simply listens. And God's listening is welcoming and weighty.

When God is silent during my prayers I'm not talking to myself. Knowing he is listening invites me to think more deeply. There with him, I realize more. The toll the mess is taking on my own heart emerges. The requirements of love come into focus. I begin to see how to move from mere moralism to God's grace. Scripture comes to my mind. Sometimes the quiet waiting forces me to settle down. In all this, God isn't really silent, of course. His Spirit speaks without making a sound.

"Even at night my heart instructs me." That's surprising, because generally my heart can be so unreliable. But the sense here is that God's counsel takes root in my heart not only when I pray but even when I sleep. The Holy Spirit sanctifies the usual sorting process of our dreams, infusing our thoughts with his clarity and wisdom.

The problems of our church and our people can become like those virtual reality headsets, so absorbing and vivid we can't see what's really true. So in prayer we resolve, "I keep my eyes always on the Lord." That is not easy, which is exactly why we pray it.

I remember a terribly difficult night when I was summoned into the middle of a toxic marriage brouhaha. It took a toll on me. I slipped into depression. At one point, as I was struggling in prayer, I cried out angrily to the Lord, "Where were you?! When I stood there and absorbed all that venom, where were you?!" And in the quiet I heard him say, just as clear as could be, "I was right by your side the whole time." Then he added, "And you did well."

And that is why "I will praise the Lord, who counsels me."

Catalytic Converters

My Dear Shepherds,

"This can't keep going on," my pastor friend told me. "I need to do something." A couple of relentless critics had worn him thin and brittle. Generally, his church was in a season of blessing despite Covid. But you know how it is. All his energy was draining into this dead sea. He called looking for some encouragement.

As it happened, I'd been thinking about David's prayer for protection in Psalm 16, "Keep me safe, my God, for in you I take refuge." My friend needed that prayer. He was in danger—not only from his critics but also from his own disoriented, souring heart. If he wasn't careful, he could do damage.

One of the ways David sought God's protection was this:

> *I will praise the LORD, who counsels me;*
> > *Even at night my heart instructs me.*
> *I keep my eyes always on the LORD.*
> > *With him at my right hand, I will not be shaken.* (Ps. 16:7-8)

Occasionally, the LORD's counsel comes as straightforward problem-solving—"do this; do that"—but not nearly so often as we'd like. I used to tell my pastoral counseling students, "Your people will come to you for counsel about marriage, kids, jobs, decisions—all kinds of things, but almost no one will ever ask you to help them with their souls. Don't let that throw you off. It's *always* about their souls." So it is when we seek God's counsel. God *always* starts with our souls.

David gave us Psalm 4 as a model prayer for the put-upon. I call it a prayer for sleepless nights. "Answer me when I call to you, my righteous God," he moaned. "Give me relief from my distress." Look at Psalm 4 yourself. It will take a good deal longer to pray those eight verses than to read them, but they're holy therapy. By the end of his prayer, David turned off his light, fluffed his pillow and whispered, "In peace I will lie down and sleep, for you alone, LORD, make me dwell in safety." Mind you, nothing in his circumstances had changed, but his heart was strong again.

Praying with our Bible in hand brings our hearts into alignment with Christ. Remember, we are invited to come boldly to God's throne of grace for his merciful help in our time of need. But we do need to *come* and not just blither out in his courtyard. There, before our merciful Father, we can find release from our guilt, the strong medicine of humility for our conflict-stiffened neck, replenishment of lost love, and the wisdom to season our words with holiness. We remember, "With him at my right hand, I will not be shaken."

It takes time to pray our souls back to health but when we do we bring Jesus' own love, grace, clarity, and holy restraint to dangerous or precarious relationships. We become *catalysts* instead of just being players. Do you recall how Peter told the wives of unsaved husbands that "they may be won over without words by the behavior of their wives, *when they see the purity and reverence of your lives*"? That works for pastors, too. Christlike character is catalytic, even without words!

My friend griped a little when I walked him through this. "This isn't what you're supposed to do when I call you," he said, chuckling. "You're supposed to tell me I'm right and they're being stupid." Then he said, "But I'm thankful that you called attention to the insensitivities in my own heart."

That's why we praise God for his counsel. Because *it's always about the soul*.

Among the Immortals

My Dear Shepherds,

Sometimes, trying to quiet our fears is like trying to tuck an octopus into bed. How many nights have you tried to sleep all tangled in your worries about the church, your family, your finances, or your own well-being? We need to know how to pray in those times because they won't let go of us unless we do. We won't be able to sing, "It is well with my soul," without prayer. It's always true, but you can't always sing it.

In Psalm 61 David prayed, "I call as my heart grows faint; lead me to the rock that is higher than I." In Psalm 16 he began, "Keep me safe, O God, for in you I take refuge." Then he prays the topography of that high rock on which we stand when we take refuge in and on God. To begin with, we do not stand alone. We are part of a holy people, "splendid friends." Plus, the Lord is our "portion and cup"—our inheritance and destiny, and he has endowed us with a bountiful and beautiful estate. What's more, the Lord himself counsels us and stands close beside us always.

Therefore, my heart is glad and my tongue rejoices.

Though our circumstances haven't changed, we have found our high rock and our song. I sign all my letters, "Be ye glad!" It's the title of a favorite song by Michael Kelly Blanchard. I chose it because I've been prone to negativity and depression so singing it is a constant reminder of just how good I have it. "Every debt that you ever had has been paid up in full by the grace of the Lord. Be ye glad!"

In David's prayer, he realized that not only was his *heart* glad but even . . .

> . . . *my body will also rest secure,*
> *because you will not abandon me to the realm of the dead,*
> *nor will you let your faithful see decay.* (Ps. 16:9-10)

Both Peter and Paul preached from this text, showing that Scripture insists on the Messiah's resurrection. For us, David's prayer comes loaded with the Easter assurance not only for *after* death but *before*. Through Christ, we have already joined a new race, the Immortals.

Paul wrote in 2 Corinthians that things had gotten so bad for him he had despaired even of life. I'm sure you remember the catalog of his suffering. You have your own catalog, maybe not so severe as his, but bad enough to leave you despairing of ministry sometimes. Who of us hasn't thought about selling shoes? It doesn't always help to look for the silver lining around some ministry struggles. What we rely upon is that the perfection of God's power really does shine brightest through our weakness. The daily dying of ministry is not our liability. Rather, as Mandy Smith says, "Weakness is a ministry resource." So add this to your praying of Psalm 16, right after verses 9-10. (Don't skim it. *Read* it.)

> *But we have this treasure in jars of clay to show that this all-surpassing power is from God and not from us. We are hard pressed on every side, but not crushed; perplexed, but not in despair; persecuted, but not abandoned; struck down, but not destroyed. We always carry around in our body the death of Jesus, so that the life of Jesus may also be revealed in our body. For we who are alive are always being given over to death for Jesus' sake, so that his life may also be revealed in our mortal body. (2 Cor. 4:7-11)*

Our confidence in the resurrection is not stored away for our dying day, but also for the dying required of us this day. You are not abandoned to your dying. You're not going to rot away. You are among the Immortals.

Pastors Go First

My Dear Shepherds,

Pastors don't have to always be upbeat, thank goodness, but we must be living displays of hope in Christ, hope here and now, and hope hereafter. We must be heavenly minded if we are to be of any earthly good. When David prayed for God's protection in Psalm 16 he described the parapets of his security, finally coming to this:

> *You make known to me the path of life;*
> *You will fill me with joy in your presence*
> *With eternal pleasures at your right hand.* (Ps. 16:11)

Pastors are pathfinders, scouts, trailmasters, exploring our God-given path of life, often out ahead of our people, so that we can better lead them. Our experiences aren't so different from other believers, but we need to be more *perceptive* about the journey than they may be. Just as the journals of Lewis and Clark gave their countrymen a sense of the treasures and wonders of the Louisiana Purchase, so pastors are to chart and describe the path of life.

"You will fill me with joy in your presence." Haven't you found that the joy of God's presence requires patience? It's not likely you will have a ten-minute prayer time and come away filled with joy. This prayer, Psalm 16, takes a good while to pray thoughtfully, but once done, joy settles in around us.

Finally, pastors must keep heaven in view—"eternal pleasures at your right hand." A vital part of our job is to make God's people homesick. Christians who never think about our "eternal pleasures" are vagabonds, hobos. Some pastors, (mostly younger ones, I suspect), almost never talk about Christ's return or heaven, thinking, perhaps, that such doctrines are for the infirm and aged, when they are actually for the soldiers of Christ. But again, we must go first in laying hold of this hope.

Our people catch homesickness from us.

In *The Pilgrim's Progress, Part 2*, Christian's wife, Christiana, along with their children, make their way to the Celestial City. They come upon "a man with his sword drawn, and his face all bloody, who tells them, 'I am one whose name is VALIANT-FOR-TRUTH. I am a pilgrim, and am going to the Celestial City.'" He becomes their rear guard lest "some fiend, or dragon, or giant, or thief, should fall upon [them], and so do mischief."

I want to be like that man. A pastor, Mr. Valiant-for-Truth, the guardian and guide of God's homeward bound pilgrims, the sword of God's Word in my hand. My favorite lines in all of literature describe what happens as this pilgrim band neared the Celestial City and this guardian hero is called home.

> After this it was noised abroad that Mr. VALIANT-FOR-TRUTH was sent for by a summons . . . When he understood it, he called for his friends, and told them of it. Then said he, "I am going to my Father's house: and though with great difficulty I have got hither, yet now I do not repent me of all the troubles I have been at to arrive where I am. My sword I give to him that shall succeed me in my pilgrimage, and my courage and skill to him that can get it. My marks and scars I carry with me, to be a witness for me that I have fought his battles, who will now be my rewarder." When the day that he must go home was come, many accompanied him to the river-side, into which, as he went down, he said, "O death where is thy sting?" And as he went down deeper, he cried, "O grave, where is thy victory?" So he passed over, and all the trumpets sounded for him on the other side.[1]

[1] John Bunyan, *Pilgrim's Progress Part 2*: Christiana, accessed online: https://www.chapellibrary.org/book/buppp2/pilgrims-progress-part-2-bunyanjohn (8-9-21), p. 107.

Homo Unius Libri

My Dear Shepherds,

Do you remember the scene in *Remember the Titans* when Coach Herman Boone drills his football team to the point of exhaustion? He walks down the row as they run in place. "What is pain?!" he shouts. "French bread!" they yell back. "What is fatigue?!" "Army clothes!" "Will you ever quit?!" "No! We want some mo'! We want some mo'! We want some mo'!" Maybe somebody should've put us through that kind of conditioning in seminary because right now, there are a lot of pastors who definitely do *not* want some mo'.

Perhaps we were prepared to bravely defend the deity of Christ or the reliability of Scripture, but I don't remember anyone ever preparing us for the sometimes exhausting, brutal, or heartbreaking work of shepherding. We had no idea.

An elder chair called me recently. Their church is without a pastor and he was at the end of his rope with fractious fellow board members. "I didn't sign up for this," he exclaimed. I sighed and said, "Well, as a matter of fact, you did."

The end of Paul's second letter to Timothy reads like one of those speeches generals give their troops before the crucial battle. "People will not put up with sound doctrine," Paul warns. "They will turn their ears away from the truth and turn aside to myths." (Is any of this sounding familiar?)

To counter these enemies both within and beyond the church Paul emphasizes one thing throughout his letter: sound teaching, grounded in Scripture. Finally, he issues these five terse commands:

> *Preach the word; be prepared in season and out of season; correct, rebuke and encourage—with great patience and careful instruction.* (2 Tim. 4:2)

Proclaim the Message with intensity; keep on your watch. Challenge, warn, and urge your people. Don't ever quit. Just keep it simple. (The Message)

Here's the problem: pressure, weariness, confusion, and sin tend to distract pastors from this primary Wordwork. Our daily duties—planning, putting out fires, meetings, reading, emails—all can be infused with Scripture, but you and I both know that they often aren't. Sometimes the Bible becomes a plaque on the wall of our work.

During the Civil War, most soldiers were issued single-shot, muzzle-loading rifles. After the Battle of Gettysburg, at least 27,574 guns were recovered from the battlefield, their owners having fled or died. *Incredibly, 24,000 were still loaded!* And half of those had been loaded *more than once*, one shot jammed on top of another, without being fired! One poor guy had apparently loaded his gun twenty-three times without ever actually shooting! Evidently fear or the chaos of battle deafened or confused them. I suspect that happens to pastors, too. When Scripture is needed most we forget to pull the trigger.

Paul approached ministry as a soldier. He told Timothy, "Join with me in suffering, like a good soldier of Christ Jesus." The weapon issued to us is Scripture, "God-breathed and useful . . . so that the servant of God may be thoroughly equipped for every good work" (2 Tim. 3:16-17). That's why I call pastors Wordworkers.

Dear shepherd, perhaps the work has become soul-deadening. Perhaps you're disoriented. Perhaps you don't know what to say or which way to turn. John Wesley, a pastor too, wrote, "O give me that book! At any price, give me the book of God! I have it: here is knowledge enough for me. Let me be *homo unius libri* [a man of one book]."

The White Line on the Side of the Road

My Dear Shepherds,

The blizzard that blew through that March night during a big high school basketball game was ferocious. Our game was 40 miles from home and there was nothing between our two South Dakota towns but banshee winds and drift-gathering hills. Our bus driver, Maynard, thought we could make it, but soon visibility turned to zero. He opened the folding entrance door and crept along, following the white roadside line for the whole trip. The 40 miles took hours. Maynard was our hero.

Sometimes ministry is like that. When we're hired we all talk about vision and goals but then comes those blizzards where we can't see a thing, our agenda is forgotten, and all we hope is to get safely home. Paul's second letter to Timothy focused on staying the course. "Proclaim the word," he told Timothy, "in good seasons and bad." Blizzards are bad seasons.

Then, Paul's last pastoral counsel to his protégé was this four-part assignment:

> *But you, keep your head in all situations, endure hardship, do the work of an evangelist, discharge all the duties of your ministry.* (2 Tim. 4:5)

That's how we follow the white line.

"Always Be Sober-Minded" (ESV). Keep your wits about you. Think before you act. Guard your tongue and your temper. My worst and costliest decisions sprang from my frustration and impulsiveness. I trusted my instincts, which sounds much better than it is. Conflict and criticism sent my internal compass spinning. I'd get angry, depressed, and sleepless. Our only safeguard is to "be strong and take heart and wait for the LORD."

"Endure Hardship." Not all beatings are measured in lashes, not all

opposition comes from Judaizers, and not all shipwrecks are at sea. You may never have "despaired of life itself" as Paul did, but surely you've despaired. Having never been taught that suffering is as much a part of ministry as teaching, we wonder when it comes if we can bail out or find a better church. But weakness is our greatest ministry secret, "for when I am weak, then I am strong." So endure.

"Do the Work of an Evangelist." Years ago I was aggravated when a guy told me he was praying that I'd get more involved in evangelism. He had no idea how much I was already doing! Nonetheless, I started hanging out at a donut shop in the mornings. In the next church it was at a bagel shop. (Not all evangelistic work happens at the Areopagus.) I made friends with people who knew nothing about Christ or his church and sometimes I got to talk with them about Jesus. What's more, I was a better shepherd of the flock having searched for the lost sheep.

"Fulfill Your Ministry" (ESV). Paul had told Timothy to "fan into flame the gift of God, which is in you," turning him from a timidity or cowardice to Spirit-given power, love, and self-discipline. Ministries run on empty, not when we're weak, but when we pretend, when we turn sour, and when the Holy Spirit no longer has our attention.

Our primary ministry task is Wordwork, always tuning into Scripture for every dilemma, need, and opportunity. Also, our ministry is to embody and dispense grace in Jesus' name to the harassed and helpless. When we are good shepherds people more easily understand Jesus.

It is frightening when we cannot see the way ahead. People are depending on us and the road is not safe. Jesus will carry us, but we must attend to our priorities: the Word, self-control, endurance, evangelism, and fulfilling our calling.

Let It Be Said of You

My Dear Shepherds,

For many years at our denomination's annual conference our ministerial association would honor the dozen or so pastors who had reached 65 years as lifetime members. I remember my admiration for those men when I was young. I would imagine all the sermons they had preached, all the meetings they had attended, and all the stresses they had faced for the Lord's sake. To me they were like old veterans who I'd see marching in the Fourth of July parade. I was proud to be in their company.

Now I am well past that milestone, so I read Paul's farewell words to Timothy with different eyes.

> *For I am already being poured out like a drink offering, and the time for my departure is near. I have fought the good fight, I have finished the race, I have kept the faith.* (2 Tim. 4:6-7)

Sometimes in ministry, if you don't look out to the time of your departure, you'll throw in the towel like a boxer signaling that he won't get back in the ring for the rest of the fight. If all you see are the meetings and the critics and the calendar, you won't make it.

A drink offering was wine poured out on a burnt sacrifice, as though the life of the sacrifice and the lifeblood of the worshipper were offered together in fellowship with God. When we share in the sufferings of Christ—taking up the cross in trust and obedience—that dying is holy, our lifeblood mingled with Christ's.

The expression, "I have *fought* the good fight," stresses the sweat-stained exertion of a runner or wrestler. "Agony" is hidden in that Greek word. Pastoring is grueling, and sometimes all you can do is push through it by the grace of God and make sure you're fighting the *good* fight and not one that matters little. We're like the Australian prizefighter years ago who wired his father after a bout, "Won easily in 84 rounds."

"I have finished the race" looks at the race*course* rather than the competition. (Contrary to our gut feeling, ministry is not competition.) I suspect if we had imagined our ministry future at all we would have pictured it as four times around a quarter mile track. Lo and behold, it was a tough and treacherous marathon! But from my aged perspective, what a privilege it was to run!

To tell you the truth, all my years I have wondered if I would be able to say at the end, "I have kept the faith." Sometimes Samson haunted me. The gospel entrusted to us will never be ripped from our grip. It doesn't happen that way. A couple of lines later Paul writes, "Demas, *because he loved this world*, has deserted me." The world winks, waggles her finger, and whispers sweet nothings, so tighten your two-handed grip on the gospel entrusted to your care.

Now I not only look back on my own ministry, I also look at you younger shepherds who pour out your lives and wrestle to exhaustion, who tackle the twisting course before you, and who are valiant for truth. Once my pastoral heroes were those older shepherds. Now they are you—today's Timothy and Titus, Phoebe and Priscilla—who come behind me; loving Christ; gripping your Bibles; learning to pray; determined to feed, lead, and guard the flocks God has entrusted to you. Dear ones, I am so proud to know you and be counted among you. And when the time of your departure comes, I will be waiting to welcome you into eternal dwellings.

Award Day

My Dear Shepherds,

When I was a full-time pastor, I often cut my grass on Sunday afternoons. It was the only time in a whole week when I got the satisfaction of *seeing* the results of my work. You know what I mean.

A young pastor interviewed me recently for his podcast. He asked me to share a story of ministry success. I was stumped because, as I told him, ministry success often comes so slowly that you can't see it. Paul might have been answering that question the last time he wrote to Timothy.

> *I have fought the good fight, I have finished the race, I have kept the faith. Now there is in store for me the crown of righteousness, which the Lord, the righteous Judge, will award to me on that day—and not only to me, but also to all who have longed for his appearing.* (2 Tim. 4:7-8)

Ministry success is measured in righteousness. We, of course, add nothing whatsoever to the righteousness of Christ imputed to us in the gospel. But once redeemed, our own righteous thoughts and deeds do matter and are rewarded by "the Lord, the righteous Judge." "The Son of Man is going to come in his Father's glory with his angels, and then he will *reward* each person according to what they have done" (Matt. 16:27).

That hard ground of tough ministerial work that Paul described—fight the good fight, finish the race, keep the faith—is the seedbed of the righteousness God grows in us. Remember Jesus' kingdom parable about the man who scattered seed? "Night and day, whether he sleeps or gets up, the seed sprouts and grows, though he does not know how. All by itself the soil produces grain" (Mark 4:27-28). Our righteousness grows as we persevere in pastoring.

The only way we can endure and keep our perspective is to "long for his appearing." Pastors, you cannot just look at what is happening around you now. Work today for that day when you will finally be able to *see* your work.

Peter wrote to faithful elders, "And when the Chief Shepherd appears, you will receive the crown of glory that will never fade away." At the end of my book, *Pastoral Graces: Reflections on the Care of Souls,* I write,

> Peter's promise of the Chief Shepherd's return assures us that pastors will not be forgotten in some lonely pasture. One day the bleating of sheep will be drowned out in the trumpet call of God. One day we will leave our last committee meeting to find ourselves in the company of angels. One day we will make our last hospital call or officiate at our last funeral and be ushered into that Kingdom where there is no more death or mourning or crying or pain. One day we will put aside our monthly reports and Sunday bulletins to take up the anthems of glory. One day we will preach our last sermons and lay aside our beloved Bibles to find ourselves awestruck in the presence of Him whose very name is the Word of God. One day we will set aside the cups and bread for the last time in order to take our places at the wedding supper of the Lamb. And when that day comes we will lay down our staffs and take our rest, for the sheep we have fed and led and guarded will be safe at last in the fold of Jesus, and we will hear, "Well done!" from the Chief Shepherd whose lambs we have loved.[1]

---

[1]Lee Eclov, *Pastoral Graces: Reflections on the Care of Souls* (Chicago: Moody Publishers, 2012), p. 170.

Sculpted

My Dear Shepherds,

A young colleague of mine told me back in April, as the pandemic settled heavily upon us, "I will not be the same pastor when this is over." An understatement, as it turns out. I know you shepherds have tried again and again to orient your hearts to God's sovereignty and perhaps you have done so without that quiet inward reassurance that the Spirit sometimes adds to bolster our faith. Such silence is the sculpting of God.

In these times, you may not have realized it but you have been sharing in the sufferings of Christ. He stood quietly at your side as you sought to trust and obey the Lord despite the darkness and the clamor. That is reason enough for praise.

> *Praise be to the God and Father of our Lord Jesus Christ, the Father of compassion and the God of all comfort, who comforts us in all our troubles, so that we can comfort those in any trouble with the comfort we ourselves receive from God. For just as we share abundantly in the sufferings of Christ, so also our comfort abounds through Christ.* (2 Cor. 1:3–5)

Christ has not been impervious to your shepherding pains and bruises from the pandemic, politics, or precautions. Jesus surely shared your heartache when you preached alone into a camera on Easter Sunday and your people sang solitary resurrection songs in their homes. He knows how you yearned for a simple Communion service, a fellowship dinner, and the embraces of your people. When you were attacked for trying valiantly to be a good shepherd he also felt the blows. It is his church, after all, and he is their Shepherd, too.

The backdrop to your prayers over these months was dark Gethsemane. Jesus knelt there with you, familiar ground to him. Nine times in

2 Corinthians 1 Paul speaks of comfort using the word *paraklesis*, akin to *paraklete*, the Holy Spirit. The God of all comfort does more than telegraph a few verses to us. *The Message* captures it:

> *He **comes alongside us** when we go through hard times, and before you know it, **he brings us alongside someone else** who is going through hard times so that we can be there for that person just as God was there for us.*

The Son of Man himself learned the one thing that the omniscient God could not know: "Son, though he was, he *learned obedience* from what he suffered..." (Heb. 5:8). You have met him in that same scarring school and he joined you as you struggled Job-like with all your aching whys. This wasting season has not been wasted on you, dear friends. You have been sculpted into comforters by the chisel of longsuffering.

In the ministry seasons ahead you will surely not be like Job's wearisome and foolish comforters. You will, in fact, be a better pastor than you once were. With your faith of higher carat gold than before, you will enrich your people by your more Christlike presence and patience, by your wisdom, grace, and trust, maybe even by your words. You have taken up your cross and thus are sculpted more closely to the likeness of Christ. That is why at this season I'm so thankful and honored to be numbered with you among the shepherds of God's flock.

Thank You, Pastors

My Dear Shepherds,

I'm thankful for pastors. I'm honored to be counted among you and love your company. I'm thankful for our unique bond; brothers and sisters in Christ, yes, but also as a band of God's own shepherds keeping watch over our flocks. I love to hear about your churches, to learn what you're preaching and what you're reading.

I love laughing with pastors. Who else has the kinds of stories we have, some we can only tell among ourselves? I love our camaraderie around our common duties. Others speak flippantly about marryin' and buryin', but we know the weight of pronouncing "husband and wife," or of marking the passage of a saint into the house of the Lord forever. We know, too, the unsettling duty of funerals for the lost. We have stories of babies and board meetings and bullies.

I'm thankful for you who preach—who lift a text there in your study, turning it in your hands, learning its weight and worth, and then standing in front of the saints, all of us so utterly ordinary, and delivering the Word of God.

I'm thankful for pastors who have borne the battle in the heat of the day, who have been wounded deeply yet not lost their love for Christ or his people. Jesus called those blessed who are insulted, persecuted, and falsely accused, and so some of you have been treated this year. I bless you in Jesus' name.

I'm thankful for pastors who feel greatly rewarded when they can open their Bibles to teach a young believer or to fortify an old one, who relish the holy privilege of introducing someone to Jesus. I'm thankful for pastors who make friends at coffee shops or health clubs, like Jesus eating gladly with tax collectors and sinners.

I'm thankful for pastors who pray, bowing unseen but by God, to beseech him to part some flood or quiet a storm, for a sermon that lies tangled on the desk, for parishioners who seem too sick in heart or body to get well; pastors whose prayers are fists against the gates of hell and who wield God's promises as the sword of the Lord; for pastors whose prayers lay open their own souls and who lose track of time when they're with Jesus.

I'm thankful for pastors in small places who have stood aching with self-doubt in some large auditorium and then gone home realizing, as R. S. Thomas wrote, "I was a vicar of large things in a small parish." I'm thankful, too, for big church pastors who are humble and who put more stock in the quality of their sheep than the size of their flock, who know that they are not mere managers of an organization but are entrusted with the household of God.

I'm thankful for pastors too young to have ever worn a suit to church and don't know their way around a hymnal like I do, yet who love Jesus, his people, and the Scriptures. I love the feel of them standing on my shoulders. I'm thankful for old pastors who, despite waning strength and war stories, are like stalwart old Caleb, willing still to face giants, if need be, in order to settle their people safely home.

So thank you, dear shepherds, for your company and your work in the Lord. Remember Galatians 6:9, "Let us not become weary in doing good . . ." (Does he *know* what he's asking?!) ". . . for at the proper time we will reap a harvest if we do not give up."

I Will Be Your Waiter

My Dear Shepherds,

We've waited so long. The night seems so deep. Our people need our constant reminders to remain at the ready. Jesus said,

> *Be dressed ready for service and keep your lamps burning, like servants waiting for their master to return from a wedding banquet, so that when he comes and knocks they can immediately open the door for him. It will be good for those servants whose master finds them watching when he comes.* (Luke 12:35-36)

So we keep watching knowing that one day he will burst through the door of the heavens, trumpet sounding. What happens next in Jesus' telling caught me by surprise.

> *Truly I tell you, he will dress himself to serve, will have them recline at the table and will come and wait on them* (v. 37).

Did you realize that Jesus washing the feet of his disciples in the Upper Room was eschatology? What shocked them we tend to take for granted. Jesus served us on the Cross. He served us when he sent the Holy Spirit, when we married into his family, the countless times he's listened as we've unburdened our hearts, and with all those answered prayers. He is constantly serving us, always washing our feet. But this?

It seems Jesus pictured us all coming into that great Upper Room, fresh from meeting him in the air, in our new immortal bodies, dressed in blood-bleached white linen. Before us is spread a vast bridal banquet, lavish and regal. The Lord, having prepared the place for us and us for the place, now invites us all to recline around the table. "On this mountain the LORD Almighty will prepare a feast of rich food for all peoples, a banquet of aged wine—the best of meats and the finest of wines" (Is.

25:6). Then, instead of taking his seat at the head of the table, the Lord Jesus lays aside his blood-dipped, gleaming white robe and golden sash to dress as a servant, and *he* begins to wait on *us*! Not just on that festive occasion but forever after! Because, after all, that is his nature.

Surely, I thought, *if Jesus' disciples had gaped to see him wash their feet, how much more dumbfounded will we be then.* But John tells us that when we see Christ we will be like him. If Jesus, even in glory, bears "the very nature of a servant," then so shall we, finally and forever. In that upside-right world, seeing our King serve will be as natural and fitting as seeing a grand coronation in this world. His service will be the very embodiment of his majesty.

But for now, our duty is to "be dressed ready for service." That is true for all believers but especially for pastors. In calling us, the Good Shepherd endowed us with love for the sheep of his pasture. That love leads to service.

Much of our service is a delight, of course, but not all of it. Pastoral service this past year sometimes seemed slavish, didn't it? It's one thing to be a servant but another to be treated like one. But for now, let us together with other shepherds, bear the slights of servitude with the grace and wisdom of Jesus. Let us wear the servant's apron like we were born to it.

Love them because Jesus first loved you. Love them because Jesus died in order to dress his bride in spotless white. Love them because by so doing we all become more and more like Jesus, and because serving them gives them a taste for heaven.

'It Will Be Good for That Servant'

My Dear Shepherds,

It is certainly easier to imagine the Apocalypse now than it was a year ago! Jesus' commands to have our people ready and waiting for his return seem more urgent. In Luke 12 Jesus told us to "be dressed ready for service . . . like servants waiting for their master to return from a wedding banquet." Peter asked, "Lord are you telling this parable to us, or to everyone?"

> *The Lord answered, "Who then is the faithful and wise manager, whom the master puts in charge of his servants to give them their food allowance at the proper time? It will be good for that servant whom the master finds doing so when he returns. Truly I tell you, he will put him in charge of all his possessions."* (Luke 12:42-44)

There is our job: To be faithful and wise managers, providing food on schedule to those in the household we oversee. Food service doesn't have the cachet of greatness or prestige but that is our job. We're quartermasters behind the lines, feeding the troops their rations. The measure of our success is a well-nourished flock, soldiers who don't wilt in battle. As Dallas Willard wrote, "Instead of counting Christians, we need to weigh them."

Pastors who love teaching the Bible sometimes assume that as long as they exposit Scripture for their people they've fed them well but, frankly, some pastors hide poor shepherding behind good preaching. We must feed our household as Jesus did, with the Word applied, visualized, and embodied by us. Pastors, breathing the Spirit, must incarnate what we preach. Most important is that our people see the love of Christ in us—in the grace we distribute like bread and the ways we wash their feet.

This isn't the best time to evaluate our work, especially not by the often-accepted metrics of pastoral success. Wait until Jesus returns for that. Feed your people now, day in and day out, meal after meal so that they are healthy, ready, and watching.

Christ's promised reward is unsettling: *". . . he will put him in charge of all his possessions."* When I read promises like that ("take charge of ten cities," is another), I think, *You know, I'm tired of being in charge of things. How about if I just sing in the choir.* But the work of heaven will be different. We may need a new word for it. "Work" is too weedy and weary. To begin with, our new responsibilities come because of the delighted trust of our Master. "Well done, good and faithful servant! You have been faithful with a few things; I will put you in charge of many things." Look at that! He's kept track of those countless small things we did in his name!

Not all our earthly accomplishments will matter then. Our pride-infected, misdirected, faithless work will have been incinerated like wood, hay, and straw. But when we did what the Lord assigned to us; when we built squarely on the foundation of Christ; when we fed, led, and guarded his flock faithfully; our humble work here will be seen there by Jesus as gold, silver, and jewels, the very building blocks of the New Jerusalem.

But there's more! Our Master will also say, "Come and share your master's happiness." Managing God's possessions in the New Jerusalem will come without weeds, without hassles. No problems to solve. No touchy people to shepherd. Everything to which we put our hand is glorious, every person is beloved, and everything is awash in the bright glory of God.

But for now, back to the kitchen.

The Alchemy of God

My Dear Shepherds,

Nick sat near me at a coffee shop patio and we struck up a conversation. He was a Vietnam vet who had suffered lifelong effects of Agent Orange. Despite being raised Catholic he told me he'd lost his faith for awhile in the war. I listened. He told me he'd sought counseling after retirement because he was so unsettled by it. I listened. When I told him I'd recently retired from pastoring, he asked me if I'd lost my faith when I retired. I was surprised by the question. "Oh no," I said, "I love Jesus. The ministry wasn't a professional duty. I love Jesus." I wonder if anyone else had really listened to him or if he'd met anyone before who really loved Jesus. When I walked away a phrase about Jesus came to my mind, "He went around doing good." *I get to do that*, I thought. All Christians can, but pastors especially.

Peter gave that summary of Jesus' ministry when he met with Cornelius and his household. He began,

> *You know the message God sent to the people of Israel, announcing the good news of peace through Jesus Christ, who is Lord of all. . . . how God anointed Jesus of Nazareth with the Holy Spirit and power, and **how he went around doing good** and healing all who were under the power of the devil, because God was with him.* (Acts 10:36, 38)

Jesus' good deeds, at least those recorded in the Gospels, were almost always miraculous. Ours don't seem to be. They seem so ordinary that I'm reluctant to put them in the Christlike category. But looks can be deceiving. What makes our good deeds Christlike is not their miracle magnitude but the Spirit's anointing upon us, the power of God at work through us, and the presence of God with us. We bring our few loaves and fish and Jesus does the rest. Remember: Jesus is in production;

we're in distribution.

I'm sure you've seen God spin the flax of some small deed to gold. The last time I visited Gwen she was so frail. It was hard for her to breathe or walk and she was sad because she had to move. After we talked a while I knelt by her side, took her hand, and prayed. When I finished she whispered plaintively, "Is there a limit to God's grace?" An old hymn came to mind so I sang it, "He giveth more grace when the burdens grow greater; . . . And out of his infinite riches in Jesus, he giveth and giveth and giveth again." When I finished, she rifled through some papers in the back of her Bible and, without a word, pulled out her handwritten copy of those very lyrics. In that gilded moment we both wept.

Sy was a sadsack kind of guy. I'd met him at a gas station where I got coffee on Sunday mornings. He'd come right out and tell me, "I'm a lost sheep." I saw him fairly often. He even came to church a couple of times and then I lost track of him. Several months later I couldn't get him off my mind so I called him. He was nearly speechless. "How did you know to call me *today*?" he asked. It was a desperate day for him. "The Lord kept bugging me to call you," I said. An ordinary call in a golden moment.

Proverbs 15:23 says, "A person finds joy in giving an apt reply—and how good is a timely word!" God's most common miracle is the divine coincidence. We bring some good deed wrapped in plain brown paper and when they unwrap it, it's gold! That's the alchemy of God.

Pockets Full of Grace

My Dear Shepherds,

I love to tell about Jim, a delightful guy from our church in Beaver Falls, Pennsylvania. He was a retired, blue collar guy who came to Christ in his 60s. My favorite memory of Jim was what he did every Sunday after the service ended. He would stuff his suit coat pockets with Smarties, those little rolls of colored candies, and all the kids would gather round him in the foyer to get theirs. "Here you go, sweetie," he'd say. He'd pat their little heads and grin. He loved the children so much that when he gave out that candy it could break your heart to watch. And we all watched.

That's a wonderful metaphor for a phrase Peter used to describe Jesus' earthly ministry: "He went about doing good." Don't you find that sometimes we're so consumed with just doing *stuff* that we forget we're entitled and empowered to "go about doing *good*"?

Often, people open doors to pastors that they usually keep closed, the way we can get into a hospital after visiting hours. Not just our church people either but even casual acquaintances. If they sense we're not in a hurry and that we'll listen they might tell us their guarded secrets or the questions they've wanted to ask God. They aren't put off if we offer to pray for them or read a couple verses of Scripture, or even if we talk to them about their sin.

We do follow in Jesus' footsteps.

> God anointed Jesus of Nazareth with the Holy Spirit and power, and **he went around doing good** and healing all who were under the power of the devil, because God was with him. (Acts 10:38)

Among Jesus' last words to his disciples was his extraordinary promise that we will do even greater works than he did because he was going to the Father and would send the Holy Spirit to be within and among us. In the very next breath, he said, "And I will do whatever you ask in my name, so that the Father may be glorified in the Son. You may ask me for anything in my name, and I will do it" (John 14:12-14). I suspect that, often, our connections with people seem so small, so routine, that we forget that the Holy Spirit might be poised to do something extraordinary.

Fred Craddock told about a pastor who made a routine hospital call. After some small talk, he bowed his head and prayed. "Oh Looord," he intoned as pastors do, "We praaay that you would raise our sister up from her bed of affliction and restore her again to your service. Amen." Then, to his astonishment, the woman swung her legs out of the bed, stood up, and walked around the room, healed! When all the fuss finally settled down the pastor went out to his car, leaned on the roof, looked to heaven, and whispered, "Don't ever do that to me again!"

The linchpin for our doing great works even through small words and deeds is the *asking* (with more faith than that guy). The measure of our good deeds is not if they rise to the status of miracles but if they extend the grace of Christ in the power of the Holy Spirit. And all we have to do is ask and believe.

Whether you give someone your undivided attention, an aptly spoken word of Scripture, unclichéd comfort, help with an errand, or a heartfelt commendation, meet people with your pockets bulging with grace.

When Faith Doesn't Know What to Think

My Dear Shepherds,

Don had been a faithful churchgoer all of his 80 years but when he came to our church his faith didn't know what to think. He waited for the sermon like a man who hadn't eaten. He'd sit right down front in rapt attention. He believed in Christ. He loved Communion more than most. But he'd had no idea how rich and life-giving Scripture was.

When Jesus appeared incognito to Cleopas and his fellow disciple on the Emmaus road they were like Don. They were deeply committed to Jesus and "had hoped that he was the one who was going to redeem Israel." But they couldn't make sense of Jesus' death or the angels' proclamation of his resurrection. Then this stranger, who had seemed oblivious to what had happened, said,

> *"How foolish you are, and how slow to believe all that the prophets have spoken! Did not the Messiah have to suffer these things and then enter his glory?" And beginning with Moses and all the Prophets, he explained to them what was said in all the Scriptures concerning himself.* (Luke 24:25–27)

Those two disciples bear a striking resemblance to folks in your church. Your people may be further down the road with Jesus than those two, but God put you among them, Bible in hand, to serve in Jesus' stead. Devout disciples—ourselves included—are still prone to be uncomprehending and slow to believe what lies plain in Scripture unless someone opens our minds.

By "foolish," Jesus meant they were undiscerning, blind to the obvious. They weren't "slow to believe" the Scriptures because they were hardhearted but because they expected too little. They thought they knew more than they did. They saw the Passover, for example, like we might study a stained-glass window at night, without ever seeing the light that made it beautiful. They knew Isaiah's Servant Songs, but evidently they had never factored them into their hopes for Jesus. Disciples are still like that, seeing only so far in Scripture, believing only so much.

I'm sure you've puzzled over why those two disciples "were kept from recognizing" Jesus. One reason is that if they'd recognized his face they wouldn't have been able to concentrate on seeing him in the Scriptures he was explaining so vividly. Incredibly, seeing Jesus in Scripture might be even better than seeing him in person! It was clearly enough to enflame their hearts.

Now, we take Jesus' place in walking with his disciples. He's there, but they just see us. So, before we meet them, we'd better study the Word diligently and prayerfully, assuming that we, too, are prone to be oblivious to what lies before us unless Jesus teaches us and we *think*, hard. Not every passage is about Jesus, but he delights to meet us in every text to show us God's grace and truth embedded there. We are not called to simply explain the Bible. We are to reveal Christ. Because when our people see Christ their hearts are set afire.

There was another guy like Don. Tom and his wife came to our church for their grandchild's dedication, and never left. It was God's Word that held them. They drank it in. Tom always sat in the second row, left side, and when I preached he just stared at me. I joked with him once, "Tom, you never take notes." He replied, "I'm not taking my eyes off you." He might have been looking at me, but in those sermons he was seeing Jesus.

Agents of Christ's Presence

My Dear Shepherds,

One evening I went to pray with some dear friends. Barb's fear over her father's declining health hung heavy in the air. We sat quietly together, heads bowed, while I tried to listen for the Lord's direction, for what he wanted me to say or pray. I was surprised when these words came: "All will be well. All will be well." When I spoke them, it was as if fresh air filled the room with relief. A few minutes later, when our time ended, Barb said, "I know Jesus is always with us, but tonight . . . he was right here in this room!"

When Jesus, risen just that morning, appeared incognito to two of his disciples on their way home to Emmaus they were kept from recognizing him. But they did see him as never before as he revealed what Scripture said about the Messiah's suffering and glory. Later they said, "Were not our hearts burning within us while he talked with us on the road and opened the Scriptures to us?"

When they reached Emmaus "they urged him strongly, 'Stay with us for the day is almost over.'" He agreed and when he came into their home and they sat down to eat, Jesus took charge, father-like.

> *When he was at the table with them, he took bread, gave thanks, broke it and began to give it to them. Then their eyes were opened and they recognized him, and he disappeared from their sight.* (Luke 24:30-31)

Surely they sat there, not only marveling how their hearts had burned earlier, but also thinking, wide-eyed, "Jesus was right here in this room with us the whole time!"

Why did Jesus vanish just at that moment? I wonder if perhaps he was preparing his disciples, teaching them that he could be with them even when they couldn't actually recognize or see him. He had told the

Eleven that he would send his Spirit to be with them, the Paraclete, the Come-Alongsider. Jesus really would be with his people always, just unseen, like he had been with the two disciples that day.

Imagine you became friends with those two, Cleopas and the other one (his wife, perhaps), a few years after this. They've told you their story often. Imagine you were talking about a passage of Scripture and they said, "Let's just be quiet and invite Jesus to meet us in these words." As you talk over what you've read, your heart begins to warm. Or they invite you for supper. When Cleopas takes the loaf of bread and give thanks, he says, "Come, Lord Jesus, be our guest." When he breaks it that bread becomes for you manna.

Pastors can be like that, Agents of Christ's Presence. We must be determined enough, quiet enough, attentive enough to wait until we know that Jesus is right here with us in the room. Pastors learn about the ministry of presence, meaning *our* presence with our people. But more important is helping people recognize *Jesus'* presence by bowing in prayer with them and waiting until Jesus has our attention. When we counsel, visit a hospital room, or lead prayer in a worship service, when we disciple someone, or pray with our leaders, we might take our cues from those two disciples who strongly urged Jesus, "Stay with us." That is a fine way to begin praying, even though they didn't realize it was a prayer at the time.

God's Gifts to Pastors: Bringing Out Treasures New and Old

My Dear Shepherds,

Perhaps, with our noses pushed so hard upon the grindstone, we might lose sight of the gifts God gives us. For one thing, he has made us a Wordworker—one among the "apostles, prophets, evangelists, pastors, and teachers, to equip God's people for works of service." Sit back for a moment and think on this gift.

Jesus schooled his disciples in the secrets of the kingdom by means of parables, those civics lessons coded as seeds and weeds, hidden treasure and a priceless pearl, and a net filled with good fish and bad.

> *"Have you understood all these things?" Jesus asked.*
> *"Yes," they replied.*
> *He said to them, "Therefore every teacher of the law who has become a disciple in the kingdom of heaven is like the owner of a house who brings out of his storeroom new treasures as well as old."* (Matt. 13:51-52)

Therein is one of God's great gifts to us Wordworkers.

This storeroom—the treasury—is our born-again heart, "its wealth and cherished values . . . understanding, personality, and very being," says D. A. Carson. What we teach does not merely come from our study. We are more than prospectors digging into the golden vein of Scripture. Through new birth our hearts become treasuries because "the knowledge of the secrets of the kingdom have been given to you" (Matt. 13:11). These aren't some cabalistic, impenetrable mysteries, but are encapsulated in the gospel proclamation, "Christ in you, the hope of glory." Now when we study the Bible, tutored by the Holy Spirit, embedded by obedience, the black and white pages are spun to gold and hidden in our hearts.

That is true for all believers because we are all called to teach and admonish one another out of the message of Christ (Col. 3:16). But Jesus' promise here heightens our understanding of the gift he has given pastors and teachers who bring his words out of the treasuries of our hearts to our brothers and sisters. A fledgling pastor's first faltering sermon is gold for those who hear, if it comes from the treasury. Yet the more we know of Scripture, the more we study it and polish our discoveries with prayer, the richer our listeners become.

John said that the Jews who heard Jesus teach "were amazed and asked, 'How did this man get such learning without having been taught?'" Later the temple guards sent to arrest Jesus returned empty-handed, their only excuse, "No one ever spoke the way this man does" (John 7:14, 46). Remember what the two disciples whom Jesus met on the road to Emmaus said, "Were not our hearts burning within us while he talked with us on the road and opened the Scriptures to us?" That is the company we keep. That is what Christ's Spirit can accomplish through us when we bring out treasures new and old.

Scripture, God-breathed, spoken through God's Spirit-filled Word-workers, gives such life to dry bones that they not only rise and walk, but become meek and merciful. They are made hungry for righteousness and then fed, made poor in spirit and pure in heart, saints who possess the kingdom of heaven and whose eyes see God.

Scripture—these treasures new and old—sculpts our souls and our churches till we take on a striking resemblance to the Lord Jesus Christ. So we say with John Wesley, "O give me that book! At any price, give me the book of God!"

Enjoy your gift!

God's Gifts to Pastors: Finding Lost Sheep

My Dear Shepherds,

I sat with a group of pastors recently and asked as I always do, "What's your favorite part about shepherding?" Michael Brandt, now a pastor to pastors, exclaimed, "Finding lost sheep!" He's not alone.

> *"And when he finds it, he joyfully puts it on his shoulders and goes home. Then he calls his friends and neighbors together and says, 'Rejoice with me; I have found my lost sheep.'"* (Luke 15:5-6)

Pastors aren't the only ones who bring people to Christ, of course, but I think we experience that gift of God differently than others do. While any thoughtful Christian would rejoice to see someone put their faith in Christ, pastors see a *sheep*, once harassed and helpless, being brought safely into the fold, being carried *home* to the flock and to our care.

New believers don't just meet Christ. They also meet Christ's body. They become part of our flock, entrusted to us by Jesus, to guard, feed, and lead. When I could introduce a new believer to our congregation on a Sunday morning they'd applaud for joy and roll out the welcome mat. The same with baptisms, hearing and seeing that testimony of new birth. Plus, pastors know the special delight and benefit of having new believers in our congregations. They refresh us all in the gospel.

Most of my time as a pastor wasn't with lost people so being around someone like Michael is good for me. He's an evangelist/pastor who served many years in church planting. Pastors like him help me remember to "do the work of an evangelist," as Paul charged us in 2 Timothy 4:5. I remember attending the crusades of Billy Graham or one of his associates and being struck with how good and invigorating it is simply to hear the gospel from a God-gifted evangelist and how wonderful to watch people coming to receive Christ.

Jesus said, "I tell you that in the same way there will be more rejoicing in heaven over one sinner who repents than over nine-ty-nine righteous persons who do not need to repent." (Luke 15:7)

I asked Michael what it is like for him to bring home a lost sheep. "Every time," he said, "I reflect on the fact that I was rescued. It is one more time when I can express my genuine gratefulness for the mercy of God in my life." He explained that his Christian parents had been heartsick over his lost condition. "I knew that when I got saved, there wasn't any greater joy in my parents' life than the joy of knowing their son was finally home." When I asked what Scripture text was most significant to him, he quoted Luke 19:10, "For the Son of Man came to seek and to save the lost." Michael said, "If the main Shepherd came to do that, maybe that's what should be at the top of my list."

In my life someone would occasionally come to Christ as a result of one of my sermons but I particularly remember the one-on-one times. It wasn't so much joy that I felt as wonder. What astonishing thing had just happened in that quiet moment, in answer to those few, fumbling words of faith? Their sins were forgiven right there before my eyes! They were made new and joined the ranks of the Immortals! Usually there was a sacred silence, sort of breathless moment, maybe with tears. And to think that while we were so subdued there in my study the angels of heaven were singing over what had just transpired before my eyes.

Oh the stories we can tell! Thank God for that gift!

God's Gifts to Pastors: Preaching Christ

My Dear Shepherds,

"Who, having been called to be a preacher, would stoop to be a king?" The Puritan, Thomas Carlyle, said that, and all God's preachers say, "Amen!"

> *We preach Christ crucified . . .* (1 Cor. 1:23)

> *For what we preach is not ourselves, but Jesus Christ as Lord . . .* (2 Cor. 4:5)

> *To preach to the Gentiles the boundless riches of Christ. . . ."* (Eph. 3:8)

I wonder if our people ever look at us on Sunday morning and marvel that such a privilege has been given to the likes of us! We well know that this royal assignment did not come to us by virtue of our qualifications but rather (I suspect) because God delights in creating *ex nihilo*.

This gift begins with our preaching staple, the evangel. I've never worn vestments but I wonder if we shouldn't be outfitted in red coats with gold buttons and braids, announced by a trumpet fanfare, and carrying a scroll which we unroll to declare, "Hear ye! Hear ye! Believe on the Lord Jesus Christ and you will be saved!"

What's more, pastors are given the honor to bring out Scripture's new and old treasures for our people, deposited in our own hearts by Bible study and prayer. I've preached 2,250 sermons so far. I never get over the fact that in Christ "are hidden *all* the treasures of wisdom and knowledge." With every sermon, we are like a jeweler, spreading diamonds on black velvet under the bright light of Christ. "No matter how many promises God has made, they are 'Yes' in Christ. And so through him the 'Amen' is spoken by us to the glory of God" (2 Cor. 1:20). That's what our sermons are: Amens to the glory of God!

Jim Bell came to our pastors' group, his face shining. In his sermon prep he'd come to Romans 5:10, "For if, while we were God's enemies, we were reconciled to him through the death of his Son, how much more, having been reconciled, shall we be saved through his life!" It was the "how much more" that stunned him.

I'll let him tell you:

> I have always been taught that the Cross was the greatest demonstration of God's love ever, and the Empty Tomb was the greatest demonstration of God's power ever, and now Paul has the nerve to suggest that they're puny compared to what is in store for me. I do not have a vocabulary to describe things being greater than the Cross, don't have an imagination that includes things greater than the Cross, but I recognize immediately (after reading the text in darkness 100 times) that Paul must be right. I am moved to speechless awe at a truth that has been right in front of me, unseen, for all my life. The Cross is the threshold leading to an infinitely greater demonstration of love and power, kept in heaven for me, overflowing into time and space for me.

Jim, being a Methodist, would sing enthusiastically Charles Wesley's hymn:

> *Happy, if with my latest breath*
> *I may but gasp his name:*
> *Preach him to all, and cry in death,*
> *"Behold, behold the Lamb!"*

Thank God for that gift to pastors!

God's Gifts to Pastors: Smallification

My Dear Shepherds,

When our son was little we'd take him to the "wooden park," one of those castle-like structures on playgrounds for kids to climb on. Problem was, he wanted me to join him and I just didn't fit very well. Too big.

> *Truly I tell you, unless you change and become like little children, you will never enter the kingdom of heaven.* (Matt. 18:3)

That change does not come naturally to anyone, I suspect, but it is essential for pastors. How can we guide others through the ladders, passages, and watchtowers of God's kingdom if we're too big? So God gives us the gift most of us don't put on our Christmas list: smallification.

This has been a year of personal pastoral downsizing. Most pastors have been deflated by inadequacy, criticism, weariness, and perhaps some flat-out failures. Some have watched helplessly as their congregations slipped away.

"We know that in all things God works for the good of those who love him, who have been called according to his purpose." One way God works for our good is by using all these smallifiers to render us kingdom-sized. Like Alice given a little vial that said, "Drink me," which shrunk her to Wonderland's scale.

But beware: all this deflation doesn't guarantee humbler pastors. All those criticisms we've borne this year can sour into grudges, resentment, conflict, and giving up. James told us, "Humble yourselves before the Lord, and he will lift you up" (James 4:10). He wrote that to believers entangled in conflicts, who under pressure were cozying up too close to the world.

Dear shepherds, I know we've been brought low, crushed even, but it is up to us to humble *ourselves* before the Lord. Our grudge isn't with the Lord, of course, nor our frustrations. We aren't weary of him. But while we were minimized by all these people and circumstances, it is before the *Lord* that we must humble ourselves. While the Magi brought gold, frankincense, and myrrh, we bring what seems like trash, this internal detritus of a terrible season gone to seed in our hearts, but that is what we must do. Bow before the King, laying our weariness, wounds, and worries before him, repenting of what these things have made of us. They brought us low, made us small, so from that low place pivot toward the Lord.

This astonishing promise awaits the smallicized: "and he will lift you up." Just as the night of Jesus' birth changed the status of shepherds forever, so it is with pastors who have co-opted the humiliations of ministry to bow humbly before the Lord. When the fight has gone out of us, when our stiff neck finally bends to Jesus, and we release our white-knuckled grip on the hurts and the controls, we will be right-sized to maneuver in God's kingdom!

Oh, to be exalted by God! What will that be like in the kingdom to come! 1 Peter 5:5 promises elders, "And when the Chief Shepherd appears, you will receive the crown of glory that will never fade away." All believers will be given crowns in heaven—signals of our reigning with Christ. I hope ours has a little shepherd's staff logo on it or something. Revelation 7:17 says, "For the Lamb at the center of the throne will be their shepherd; he will lead them to springs of living water. And God will wipe away every tear from their eyes." If Jesus remains our Chief Shepherd forever, I wonder if somehow we might continue to shepherd with him. That would be honor enough.

Until then, glory to God in the lowest!

Made in USA - Crawfordsville, IN
17653_9781614072478
09.21.2022 1505